Anna

Here are all the angels
you will ever need!
Get well soon
love
Christiane x y
June 2001.

The Angelic Year

The Angelic Year

Healing Through Angelic Meditation

Ambika Wauters

CARROLL & BROWN PUBLISHERS LIMITED

First published in 2000 in the United Kingdom by

Carroll & Brown Publishers Limited
20 Lonsdale Road
Queen's Park
London NW6 6RD

Deputy Art Director Tracy Timson
Editor Geoffrey Chesler
Art Editor Gail Jones

Copyright © 2000 Carroll & Brown Limited
Text copyright © 2000 Ambika Wauters

A CIP catalogue record for this book is available from the British Library.

ISBN 1-903258-09-X

Reproduced by Master Image Pte Ltd, Singapore
Printed and bound in Italy by MILANOSTAMPA

Reprinted 2001

Angels are perfect spiritual beings who mediate lovingly between God and humankind.

Contents

Introduction

Angels are perfect spiritual beings who mediate lovingly between God and humankind.

Angels are the channel of our ever-present connection with God, whose mission is to guide us on our spiritual path. God loves us, and created us in His likeness, to know and love Him through loving ourselves. His Divine spark lives in each of us. Turning that spark into a flame, to burn away everything that is unlike love, light, or truth, is the work of angels.

Angels act as God's messengers to humankind, and provide the means by which our dreams are realized and our hopes fulfilled. They encourage healthy attitudes to life, self-acceptance, and gratitude. They help us to stay flexible, positive, open to new possibilities, and receptive to the miracles they bring daily into our lives.

There are angels whose purpose is to serve humanity throughout its evolution. The most powerful of God's messengers, these are the archangels, who provide us with protection, healing and guidance; they can be summoned to help us in both our individual and our collective needs. The archangels can be called upon when we are hurt or lost. They return us to our spiritual roots, working with our guardian angels to provide whatever is needed for our souls' learning and growth. They offer us the word of God, and they encourage us to let our own light shine and heal the world.

Angels in Our Lives

It is believed that angels operate in our lives by stimulating our minds and imaginations. They whisper the good word in our ears, and sharpen our perceptions of the world. They teach us that we already know the correct place to be, as well as our path toward it. The answers to our questions lie within us.

Angels provide us with many of our insights. We often call this inspiration or enlightenment, little realizing that we are actually taking the light of consciousness that they provide and calling it our own. We are divinely inspired, and it is the angels who carry our spirits up into the realms of higher consciousness.

Angels are at present encouraging our transformation from a materialistic society into one with a more refined, spiritual state of awareness. They are helping us to

8

process the rapid changes that society is undergoing. If we allow them into our consciousness—and they are only waiting to be asked—they will transform us into more honest, loving, and dedicated people.

Angels help us to make healthy and wholesome choices. They steer us toward those people and situations that further our psychological growth and spiritual development. They know what we can't yet see or sense about ourselves—that we are all children of God—and their intention is to remind us of this every moment.

If we recognize this fully, our lives begin to work in remarkable ways. We actually become partners with the angels in

all they ask of us, and that is how their unconditional love works, supporting us in trying and difficult times. They help us to stretch ourselves and to realize our dreams.

Working with Angels
Many people ask how they can get in touch with the angelic realms. To do this requires an open mind and a clear intention to reach levels of attunement with the heavenly fields where angels dwell. Yet, whether we realize it or not, we are always connected to them, and by them to God, and they know our every prayer.

The angels are the agents of God's eternal love for us. They love beauty, simplicity, cleanliness, candlelight, integrity, spiritual thinking, and joy. They enjoy celebration, and respond to gratitude. They patiently await our request for healing, love, and light.

Our souls have always known that they are called to gather their highest truth. Angels help us to clear away negativity, and gain insight into attitudes that limit us. As we take responsibility for ourselves, for the patterns of unloving attitudes, abuse, cynicism, and self doubt, we begin to see the need for a strong and viable spiritual context in which to place our experiences.

Most of us have a sense of lack or unworthiness. We need help in resolving this, in finding the precious jewel of the Self at our innermost core. At this deep level we know our innate worth as loving and worthwhile beings, but to learn the lesson of who we truly are takes many

creating a joyful and fulfilled life for ourselves. They are our support team, encouraging us when we are low, cheering us when we win, and helping us to celebrate the miracle of life.

Their presence helps us to find our grit, to stand tall in the face of adversity, and to do the best we can in any situation. That is lifetimes. The angels have helped us through this process from the beginning of our spiritual journey to the present.

We can seek their help through prayer, meditation, affirmation, and visualization. We can begin working with them by taking responsibility for what we feel and need. In doing so, we surrender our fears and doubts to God, and entrust our hopes and dreams to Him. This enables His angels to work on our behalf. Being clear about our desires helps them to help us.

As we direct our thoughts and prayers, our hearts and minds open to the power within us that realizes our intentions. The angels remind us that we are not only worthy, but infinitely capable of creating that which we long for. Peace, love, and happiness are always available to us. There is no price for this. We are worthy of love, kindness, and respect simply because we exist. This comes with being human.

Angels Offer Us Protection

There are well-attested stories about angels protecting soldiers, policemen, and large crowds of people in peril. There are also accounts of remarkable healings, both officially affirmed and unofficially acknowledged, that confirm the universality of angelic intervention.

It is said that our guardian angels have lived with us since the beginning of our souls' journeys through time. They never abandon us, criticize us, or blame us. They require only that we be aware that they are near, waiting to be summoned to provide

hope, encouragement, and even humor. The reports of angelic intervention show that they are very close to us at all times.

We can also call on them to help other people in trouble. You will be amazed at how instantly the energy shifts and healing comes to soothe or assist those who are in need. Angels love to answer a prayer. That is, after all, their function.

Angels in Times of Trouble

Angels assuage our grief, stop us being fearful, and limit our unhappiness. They reassure us that no matter what happens to us, we are always loved, guided, and protected. Our spirit cannot die or be lost. Nor can we, in truth, fail. We are always provided with another opportunity to learn, and our souls are given the experience they need for development.

Sometimes our pain can be so intense, or a separation so final, that we cannot see the higher purpose. And yet, with time, circumstances unfold to reveal the key that unlocks the door to the next stage of our lives. Sometimes we come to know in hindsight that we have only been able to transcend a difficulty because we were given the grace and love of a higher source.

Knowing the angels is not conditional on mystical thinking. It simply needs the acceptance that we may not have all the answers, and that there are things out of the bounds of everyday life that affect and influence us. Angels fit into the category of imponderables. They are an aspect of the mystery of how the Holy Spirit moves.

How to meditate, pray, and visualize

We can deepen our communion with God and the angels through prayer, meditation, and visualization. These techniques are offered here to reanimate your imagination, to stimulate your faith, and to help you to reflect on different themes. Take time to explore each activity. Be kind to yourself, especially if you are unfamiliar with these ways of approaching your inner world. You will find that, with practice, you will feel more comfortable communicating with God in this way.

Meditation
Meditation is a receptive form of communion with the Divine. Find the time to still your mind of its endless chatter. Relax your body, breathe gently, and listen intently to the nothingness that is within you. This will calm your emotions and enable your body to stop pumping adrenaline. Let go of conscious thought and go deep within yourself. It is said that God lives within your heart and reflects His light into your higher mind. When you are still you can experience this.

You may find that there are meditations that delight you and give you a feeling of peace and ease. Others might stimulate you to think about your life, or the quality of your present situation. Yet other meditations may evoke memories that reactivate old wounds, losses, and traumas. If this occurs, allow the energy of these past events to run its course and pass out of your consciousness. Use whatever comes to you in meditation as guidance for where you need to be now.

Prayer
Prayer has been described as the active form of communion with God. In prayer, either silent or vocal, we talk to our Heavenly Father, opening our heart, sharing our pain, asking for help, and expressing our deepest gratitude.

Prayer is the expression of our deepest longing for wholeness and happiness. The ability to pray comes from the knowledge that we are not alone, or expected to experience life without help. Testaments to the healing power of prayer are universal. We have all heard stories about miraculous answers to prayers. Prayer will connect you immediately to the Source, and be the pillar of your relationship with God.

You may already have special prayers that you are used to saying. The prayers in this book can be used to augment your own. Prayers do not need to be fancy or eloquent for God to hear us: some believe that He knows our requests long before we verbalize them. Rather, prayer helps us to focus our gratitude, and clarify our intent. It is our eternal connection with God, and it brings our message home to the Source.

If you are unfamiliar with prayer, use those in this book until you can find your own words when communicating with God. It gets easier with practice. Let the words come from your heart and express what is true for you.

The act of prayer allows you to go to the depth of your soul and discover what truly matters. If you are doubtful about the efficacy of prayer or feel that you are not being listened to, you might try asking for a sign or message to let you know that your prayers have been received. God wants the channel of communication to be open.

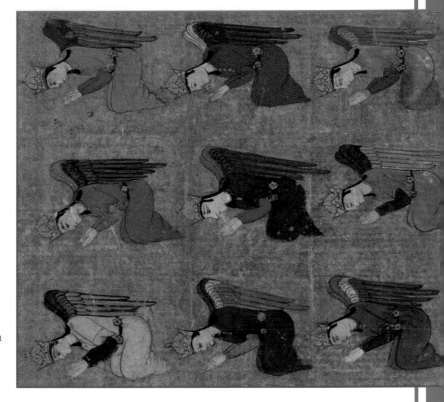

Visualization

This is a way of training the imagination to envisage wholesome results and optimal situations to enhance your life. When you see something in your mind's eye, it gives you power to manifest it. Try strengthening your imagination by practicing seeing color and forms with your inner eye. This is a beginning to mastering visualization.

Visualization has been used to help patients shrink tumors, and by athletes to improve their performance. We are using it in meditation in order to stimulate our spiritual consciousness.

Like developing a muscle, reactivating a long dormant imagination will take time and practice. Once you can see what you want in your mind's eye, you can invest your emotions in it. When you release this creation into a prayer, the heavens will know exactly what you are requesting. There is no way that the blueprint can fail to materialize if you visualize clearly what it is that you want.

How to use this book

The Angelic Year takes its structure from the Jewish and Christian calendars, following the cycles of the zodiac from the beginning of spring, with the vernal equinox in the sign of Aries, to the end of winter, in the sign of Pisces. It features the essential religious holidays that highlight the Divine Presence in our lives.

The four great archangels rule the changes of seasons, and in some cases preside over holidays. They are so luminous that their light covers the energy of an entire season, and they govern the themes of the signs of the zodiac. Each sign of the zodiac is ruled by an angel who exemplifies its distinctive archetype. The seventeen angels of the festivals help us to draw close to God's grace at significant times of the year.

There are fifty-two angels for the weeks, and each is allotted a theme that accords with the growth and healing of its ruling sign and season. These are devoted to expanding our consciousness, and to enhancing our experience of change.

Angels help us to integrate the seasonal and human cycles of change, giving a broader, organic meaning to our personal transformation. We each have our own individual cycles of development, which they see us safely through. The signs of the zodiac, seasons, and holidays help us to grow within the wider context.

This is a book for all states of consciousness and levels of development. Use it for your personal needs, share it with friends and family. Honor those moments of change, transition, and celebration. As you follow the cycles of the zodiac and festivals, note which angels resonate most closely with you. Let the consciousness of each angel work in your body, mind, and spirit, so that you integrate its essence into your being. You will actually start to resemble that angel as you become lighter, freer, and more open to experiencing the light and love of God.

Use This Book Any Time of the Year
You can use this book at any time of the year. Simply find the angel of the season, the angel of the zodiac, and of the week of that sign, to tap into the guidance, love, and protection that they offer us. This book is for the good times in your life, when you wish to celebrate; it is also for those periods of transition, when you are caught up in change and turmoil.

Open This Book Using Synchronicity
Another way to use this book is to open it at random and read the angelic prayer. This

may be just what you need to hear at the moment. Let the synchronicity of the angel you choose bring you insight and understanding. This is a wonderful way to hear the word of God resonating with your inner reality. It helps you to become aware that messages and signs are always there to give you guidance and protection.

Find What You Seek
A third way of using the book is to let it help you integrate a particular quality or emotional experience into your life. Look at the table of contents, and find the angel that corresponds to the quality you seek. It can help to clarify your emotions, strengthen your resolve, and sustain you through the moments when your shadow dominates the landscape of your spirit.

In this book, angels act as signposts for our development, and as torchbearers who light our ways to greater illumination. Let them guide your spirit and support your projects and dreams. If you are truly open to your needs, and express them with intent, they will give you the strength and courage to turn your deepest wishes into reality.

The Festivals

The traditional festivals of Judaism and Christianity give us the opportunity to celebrate the Divine Presence in our life, and to welcome in the Holy Spirit to bless us.

These are portal days, in which the veil between heaven and earth is thin, and the essence of the Holy Spirit and the realm of angels is more easily within our understanding. Our awareness of God is stronger, and the sanctuary of love and peace He offers is closer to our hearts.

17

EASTER

The oldest and holiest festival in the Christian calendar, Easter is presided over by the Angel of Resurrection. For millions of believers, the greatest miracle and the most powerful event in history is the resurrection of Christ from his tomb three days after after his death on the cross. It is the central mystery of the Christian faith.

Between March 21 and April 25 in the West; between April 3 and May 8 in the East

*E*aster is known as "the feast of feasts." This joyous celebration of Christ's victory over sin and death signifies rebirth, renewal, and the hope of eternal life. As the ancient legend of the phoenix rising from the ashes tells the story of passion and rebirth, so Christ's resurrection brings our faith in providence to a new level of refinement and understanding. We see the mystery of creation revealed to us anew each spring when new life emerges.

At a deep psychological level, the story of the resurrection suggests the need for the human soul to forgive, to learn to release its baggage, and to be born again. Easter offers us the promise of perpetual spiritual renewal.

We are resurrected in the eternal light of the spirit when we celebrate who we truly are at core. As death is a falling away of what no longer has life, so we are able to release all that no longer serves our conscious development as spiritual beings. By surrendering our ego to the higher mind and letting our self-importance die, we learn to be resilient and courageous.

The resurrection shows us that we have the opportunity to rise above pain, pettiness, loss, and separation. It helps us to find our heart again. This is the miracle of Easter.

MEDITATION

Reflect on your willingness to love and accept every aspect of yourself. Be willing to embrace every situation unconditionally, as Christ did at his death. You will find the grace to forgive all that seems unworthy in yourself. Accept the side of you that hungers for love, tenderness, and respect as part of your nature. You can find it in your heart to love yourself as your Father in heaven loves you. In this way, you resurrect your spiritual nature.

Prayer

*Beloved Angel of
Resurrection,
we offer our prayers
to God to raise up our
awareness and
to show us the glory
of our Higher Self.
Help us to transcend
pain, humiliation,
mortification, and
even death,
to know the Perfect
Jewel that we are.
Help us to transcend
our grievances.
Enlighten our minds
to know our souls'
need for love
and peace.
Help us to shine
and rise above all
limitations to our
fullest expression.
Amen.*

19

PASSOVER

The Angel of Redemption rules the Jewish festival of Passover, the joyful commemoration of the dramatic Exodus of the Israelites from Egypt. It celebrates not only freedom from physical slavery, but the liberation of the spirit from the shackles of the ego.

Nisan 15–22 in the Jewish calendar;
in late March–April

*P*assover (in Hebrew, *Pesach*) is one of the three ancient pilgrim or harvest festivals, when Jews would flock to the Temple in Jerusalem to worship. It is the festival of freedom, celebrating God's deliverance of Israel from slavery in Egypt, and looking ahead to the redemption of the world from sin in the messianic age.

This joyous Jewish festival marks the covenant between God and His people to uphold His Laws and live in freedom. It is a time to celebrate our personal and political freedom to live in accordance with our consciences, to do, think, and pray as suits our spirit. It reminds us all that the primary life principle, "I am that I am," revealed to Moses in the burning bush, expresses itself in each person in a unique form. We respect the freedom of individuals to redeem their spirit in their own way.

The life principle is the Divine spark within each of us that grows with the experience of freedom and self-expression. As we celebrate this holiday, we consciously redeem our souls from the bondage of materialism, greed, lust, emotional dysfunction, and anything that impedes our development as whole individuals. We offer our prayers to God to be born anew in spirit.

MEDITATION

In your still moments, explore those parts of you that feel disconnected from your deep center. Redeem what you have disowned in yourself. Find the vitality and power that resonates in each cell of your body. Call back your life energy with each breath. You can do this meditation at an emotional level, reclaiming such qualities as goodness, strength, and courage. Redeem whatever you have let die within you, on any level of your being.

Prayer

*We pray to you,
O Angel of
Redemption,
to assist us in calling
back the lost parts
of our Spirit.
Please redeem that
which we have lost
in ourselves
in the hope of finding
love, friendship, and
happiness.
We ask that we be
reconnected with the
I AM THAT I AM,
and learn to trust
that deepest core
of Self within.
Restore us to
wholeness
and integrity.
Amen.*

21

PENTECOST

The Angel of Gratitude presides over the Christian festival of Pentecost, which celebrates the gift of the outpouring of the Holy Spirit upon Jesus' disciples, transforming them into apostles of the new faith. We give thanks on this holiday for the transforming power of God's love in the world.

*T*he Christian season of Pentecost (Greek for "fiftieth day"), concluding on Whit Sunday, corresponds to the Jewish Feast of Weeks, which falls on the fiftieth day after Passover. When the disciples had gathered in Jerusalem for this festival, the Holy Spirit descended on them in tongues of fire, transforming them into the Church of God, charged with proclaiming Christ's message to the world. Pentecost is thus the second most important festival in the Christian year, after Easter, known as "the birthday of the Christian Church."

Reception of the Holy Spirit created a state of ecstasy in the disciples, causing them "to speak with other tongues." They found the communication skills that would enable them to speak to people in their own languages, and the courage to face danger when spreading the Gospel abroad.

This holiday reminds us of the power of change and transformation. At this time of year, nature is turning her shoots and blooms into fruit, in an alchemical process that involves the transmutation of life energy. The life force is firmly embedded in the earth, and as nature unfolds before our gaze, we bear witness to the power of change, and offer thanks to God for the miracle of life that sustains us and allows us to grow and thrive.

MEDITATION

List in your mind the things for which you are grateful. You can begin with thanks for the people around you who cherish and support you. Their prayers for your health and happiness make a difference to your well-being and peace of mind in times of transition. Give thanks for the love that sustains you, for the people who believe in you and are on "your side." Give thanks for the opportunities you have to express yourself freely, and for your thoughts, feelings, and creative expression.

Prayer

*Blessed Angel of
Gratitude,
be a constant
reminder of our need
to offer thanks to the
Creator for our life.
Let our prayers
acknowledge the
beauty, abundance,
care, and fostering
that are bestowed on
us each day.
Let us count our
blessings,
and give thanks to
the Divine Mercy
that accepts our flaws
and loves us
unconditionally.
Amen.*

23

SHAVUOT

Sivan 6–7; in May–June

The Jewish Feast of Weeks, celebrating the giving of the Law of Moses at Sinai, is ruled by the Angel of Strength. This is the core event of Jewish history, when a group of simple nomads was imbued with moral strength and a sense of purpose by their acceptance of God's Covenant.

*S*havuot (literally "weeks"), or the Jewish feast of Pentecost, is another of the three biblical pilgrim or harvest festivals. It falls seven weeks after the second day of Passover. Originally tied to the dedication of the wheat harvest, it is now mainly celebrated as the time when the Ten Commandments were revealed to Moses on Mount Sinai and engraved upon two tablets of stone.

On Shavuot, synagogues and temples are decorated with flowers and plants, recalling that the barren mountain bloomed when God revealed His Law. Mystical Kabbalists hold a vigil on the night before Shavuot, as a preparation for the spiritual marriage between Israel and God implicit in the Covenant at Sinai.

By freely accepting the gift of God's Grace, the people of Israel were transformed and strengthened. Strength can be defined physically, as having the muscle to manage heavy tasks demanding stamina or brute force. Emotional or spiritual strength, however, calls for another type of muscle. It is part of the internal process of accepting both pain and pleasure, an acceptance that springs from the experience of love. A loving heart and nurturing nature will give you the strength to survive difficult and challenging times.

Cultivating spiritual strength requires an understanding of the universal laws. This means that when tragedy strikes, or life is not optimal, we have the grace and grit to look within and to learn from these events. This type of strength is aligned to the higher purpose of God's plan, and is not anchored in our small will or ego. This ancient Jewish holiday reaffirms the strength of our intimate connection to the Divine.

Prayer

Blessed Angel of Strength,
be our shield
when life presents us with challenges.
Fortify us to endure the hard times.
Give us stamina for the long haul,
and grace to enjoy the precious moments
of freedom and wonder.
Let our strength also know the places
where we are frail and weak,
and find compassion for these parts
of ourselves.
Amen.

MEDITATION

Reflect on your weaknesses. This is the path to discovering your strengths. Begin by asking yourself how strong you are in meeting the tasks of your everyday life. See if your emotions are stable, and if you can rise to the challenges that test you. Affirm your faith in God to see you through whatever trials you face. Strengthen this connection with prayer and meditation. Put your faith in His eternal strength to be your fortress.

25

ST. JOHN'S FEAST

St. John's Feast, so near the summer solstice, is presided over by the Angel of Illumination. It celebrates the birthday of the prophet who, as a brilliant spiritual light, foretold the coming of the Lord. This time of greatest light links God, man, and nature in the unfolding year.

June 24

The birthday of Saint John the Baptist falls on Midsummer Day, just after the summer solstice. John's father, Zacharias, was a priest, and his mother, Elizabeth, was a cousin of the Virgin Mary. His remarkable birth in their old age was foretold by an angel.

John became an ascetic preacher in the Judean wilderness, calling upon sinners to repent and purify themselves by baptism in preparation for the Kingdom of God. He recognized Jesus as the promised Messiah, and baptized him in the River Jordan.

This feast links the spiritual light of the prophet, who foretold the coming of Christ, to the brilliance of the longest day. As the days begin to shorten after this high point, so John accepted that his influence would wane as that of the Lord increased.

Bonfires and feasts on Midsummer Day are traditional in many countries; they remind us of the power of the sun to illuminate our day, and of the light of higher consciousness to illumine our minds. This festival celebrates the power of our own inner nature to suffuse life with Divine light all year long.

MEDITATION

Allow yourself to feel the intensity of your inner spirit. Let it manifest itself in your awareness of life around you, and radiate out toward all who need comfort, wisdom, and healing. You have the ability to bring these qualities to your particular corner of the planet. Trust your inner light to guide you to the hearts and minds of people who will value you, and who will encourage your light to shine brightly.

Prayer

*Beloved Angel of
Illumination,
open our eyes to the
Divine Light within
ourselves,
to the radiance that
lives at our core.
Let us know how
brilliant our spirit is,
and allow us to share
our goodness
in the best ways that
we can.
We honor this day of
light in which the
spirit of God is at its
most illuminating.
Shine your light upon
us, and bless us all
with enlightened
hearts and minds.
Amen.*

THE ASSUMPTION OF THE VIRGIN

The feast of the Assumption of the Blessed Virgin Mary is presided over by the Angel of Grace. The gift of God's grace to the compassionate Mother of Christ, who intercedes on our behalf in heaven, offers the hope of salvation to millions of ordinary people whose lives may seem hopelessly compromised.

This feast, in honor of the miraculous assumption of the Virgin Mary directly into heaven, is an ancient and widespread devotion in the Roman Catholic and Orthodox Churches. As Mary was born without original sin, so she passed from this life without suffering the corruption of death, which is the result of sin. Having been taken up body and soul into the glory of heaven, she anticipated the destiny of all just believers. Thus, the opening prayer of her Mass ends with the words, "May we see heaven as our final goal and come to share her glory."

The universal outpouring of devotion to the Blessed Virgin Mary on this sacred day is presided over by the Angel of Grace.

It is a heartfelt celebration of wholeness and healing. When we open our hearts to love, and ask for the grace of the Blessed Virgin Mary to intercede for us and to hear our prayers, we come closer to loving the maternal spirit within ourselves.

MEDITATION

Draw your attention inward, and release all thoughts that clutter your mind. Imagine your heart as a shining, golden light representing the essence of God within you. Intensify this light to embrace all your love. Let it penetrate your body, mind, and spirit. Let it radiate out toward the world, opening up the dark corners of people's hearts and minds where love does not shine. This grace is a manifestation of your connection with the Holy Spirit, and comes from a caring and loving heart.

Prayer

*To the beloved Angel
of Grace, who shines
her light upon the
face of all who
ask for love.
Teach us that you are
never far from us,
ready to be invited
into our hearts.
Help us to accept our
lives with grace,
and to share the best
of our light.
We all hunger for the
deep, rich experience
of living in the
presence of God
and with the blessing
of the Holy Spirit.
Allow your grace to
shine within our
hearts and minds.
Amen.*

MICHAELMAS

Michaelmas is the feast day of St. Michael the Archangel, traditionally the defender of Christians against the heathen, and guardian of the soul, especially at the hour of death. In the early Church, in Asia Minor, he was venerated as a healer. In the West, his festival celebrates the dedication of a church in Rome in his honor.

The Angel of Justice is a powerful form of the Archangel Michael. In this role he is the Divine representative of all goodness and light, who stands for the integrity of the Holy Spirit. He triumphantly fights for the rights of mankind and defends all who are downtrodden.

Michael is usually portrayed as holding a sword in his right hand and a pair of scales in his left hand. In the scales, he weighs the souls of those who pass into eternity, to examine whether they have developed their spirits in this lifetime and grown through their struggles. Michael judges whether each soul has honored its contract for consciousness and negotiated with its guardian angel before its incarnation on earth.

Michael stands here for eternal justice, for the fulfillment of all karma, and for God's promise to honor His covenant with mankind. Michael is the living presence of the integrity of that promise. He is the Holder of the Keys of Heaven, the Prince of the Presence, the Angel of Penitence, of Righteousness, Mercy, and Sanctification, and the Angelic Prince of Israel.

Michael is the leader of the heavenly armies and defender of all who wish to know the merciful Presence of the Lord. He is the angel who rules over the Catholic Church, the police, soldiers, and lawyers. He is often shown slaying the dragon, which represents negativity, unconsciousness, and evil, and he protects all who seek his grace.

Michael represents that aspect of our Self that springs from our highest principles. He stands for the true Warrior within, whose courage, fortitude, and integrity pervade all actions and deeds. He teaches us, through his strength, how to triumph over adversity, and shows us how to clear away old, negative attitudes.

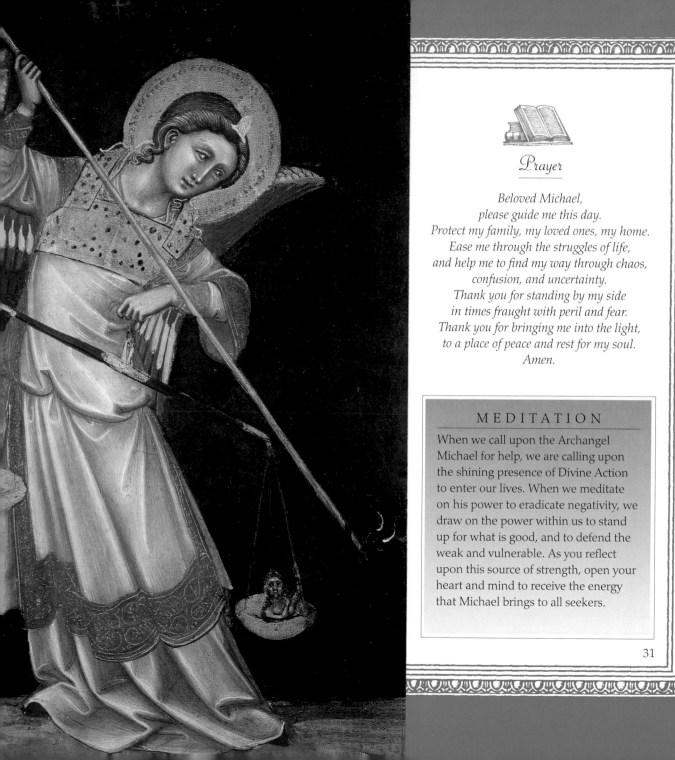

Prayer

Beloved Michael,
please guide me this day.
Protect my family, my loved ones, my home.
Ease me through the struggles of life,
and help me to find my way through chaos,
confusion, and uncertainty.
Thank you for standing by my side
in times fraught with peril and fear.
Thank you for bringing me into the light,
to a place of peace and rest for my soul.
Amen.

MEDITATION

When we call upon the Archangel
Michael for help, we are calling upon
the shining presence of Divine Action
to enter our lives. When we meditate
on his power to eradicate negativity, we
draw on the power within us to stand
up for what is good, and to defend the
weak and vulnerable. As you reflect
upon this source of strength, open your
heart and mind to receive the energy
that Michael brings to all seekers.

31

ROSH HASHANAH

The Jewish New Year celebrates God's compassion, and initiates a time of self-assessment and resolution. It is presided over by the Angel Israel, who represents the Word of God. On this day, he helps us to step out of our everyday lives in order to assess our development over the past year and to take responsibility for the future.

Tishri 1; in September–October

*R*osh Hashanah (Hebrew for "head of the year") is the Jewish New Year festival, and the first of the Days of Awe. Rosh Hashanah's date in the Jewish calendar, the first day of the month of Tishri, is thought to have been when God created Adam. It is also called the Day of Judgment, because it ushers in ten days of penitence and soul searching, during which time God judges us and determines our fate for the year that lies ahead. The name of each individual is inscribed in one of three books open in heaven: one for the truly righteous, one for the wicked, and one for those in between.

In a demonstration of trust in God's compassion, Jews celebrate Rosh Hashanah with joy. Honey is eaten, to guarantee a sweet year. White, the color of purity, is worn in temples and synagogues, and the *shofar*, or ram's horn, is sounded to awaken the soul.

The Angel Israel, who rules this festival, is a member of the *hayyoth*, the distinctive class of angels surrounding the throne of God who call upon the heavenly hosts to chant His praise. He is identified with the Logos, or the word of God, whose transforming power he demonstrates.

On this high holy day we turn our energy inward, to honor and enhance our spiritual light. This is a time to set aside worldly concerns, to gain strength, inner nourishment, and clarity of purpose. We reflect on our relationship with God, with our brothers and sisters, and, especially, with ourselves.

The Angel Israel supports our efforts to develop and grow in grace. He shows us the power of God to participate in our lives, making them richer and more fulfilling. With his help, through self-knowledge, we derive a sense of our inner worth, and discover that the power to fulfill our destiny is within our hands.

Prayer

*We pray to the Angel Israel to grant us
understanding of our worth,
and to help us to find guidance on how
to live by our inner light.
We pray to release anger and frustration,
and to heal hurt and feelings of shame.
We pray for a fuller knowledge of life,
and to balance the quest of our spirit
with the aspirations of our ego.
Amen.*

MEDITATION

Recall those occasions over the past
year when you may have been
disconnected from your inner core.
Trust in this core of Self to illuminate
the limitations, fears, and negative
patterns that are impeding your
spiritual development. Reflect on the
times you have limited yourself, and be
willing to expand to higher levels of
consciousness in the year to come. The
Holy Spirit will come to a penitent and
loving heart.

YOM KIPPUR

Yom Kippur is the holiest day of the Jewish year. This solemn day of atonement, when the faithful repent their sins, is marked with prayer, abstinence, and fasting. It is ruled by the Shekhinah, the compassionate, feminine aspect of the Godhead, who holds out the hope of redemption through love and moral change.

Tishri 10; in September–October

Yom Kippur (Hebrew for "Day of Atonement") is the most sacred day in the Jewish year. It marks the end of the ten days of penitence and is observed with a twenty-five-hour fast. Atonement refers to the reconciliation of God and man, which is attained through repentance, prayer, charity, and good deeds.

Although it is a day of awe, Yom Kippur is based upon the certainty of God's compassion. It is believed that the quality of God's forgiveness is five hundred times greater than His anger. God wants to forgive. He is merciful, gracious, and long-suffering, and it is our duty to imitate Him by being prepared to forgive others.

Yom Kippur is thus governed by the spirit of the Shekhinah, who represents the feminine face of the Divine. She is "the angel which redeemed me from all evil" in Genesis 48:16, and the liberating angel of Exodus 23:40. When you invoke the Shekhinah on Yom Kippur, you call your destiny into your hands. At that moment all that you have been and can be is laid before you, enabling you to choose your path with responsibility and humility. As you pray to this most powerful force, ask for the grace to accept God's plan, and to fulfill the promise of your Divine potential.

MEDITATION

Reflect on your path in life, and consider what aspect of it needs transformation. Is there an area where you are not fully able to be yourself, or where you feel unfulfilled? Choose to free yourself from ties that do not honor you, or do not allow you to develop to your highest capacity. This is a moment when the path you choose will affect your destiny. Ask the Shekhinah to help you find the way. When we surrender to the will of the higher power, change comes gently and subtly.

34

Prayer

*Beloved Shekhinah,
Bride of God,
unite the fragments of
our souls so that we
may live and love in
wholeness.
Let us honor the
contracts made to
heal, love, and be the
best that we can.
Redeem us, bring us
back to your bosom,
hold us close, and
renew our power,
strength, and
integrity.
Let our spirit heal
the wounds of
separation.
Let us honor the
female within us all
who knows that she
is worthy and noble.
Amen.*

Prayer

*Beloved Angel of
Permanence,
teach us to
differentiate between
what is truly lasting
and what is just a
passing glimpse of
reality.
Help us to identify
the bedrock of our
souls, and not the
fleeting waves
washing over us.
This way we keep our
sight on what is true
within us.
Help us to value
what is permanent
within,
and what has lasting
and sustainable
worth in this world of
constant change.
Amen.*

36

SUKKOT

Sukkot, the Jewish Feast of Tabernacles, is governed by the Angel of Permanence. The wandering Israelites were rewarded by admission into the Promised Land, symbol of God's providence toward those who put their trust in Him. The only safe haven in a world of conflict and change is the love of the Lord working within our hearts.

*S*ukkot (Hebrew for "Tabernacles") is one of the three Jewish pilgrim or harvest holidays. It is the happiest of the biblical festivals, celebrating God's bounty and protection, symbolized by the fragile booths or tents that the Israelites lived in during their wanderings in the desert. During the seven days of Sukkot, devout Jews eat and live in such booths, or tabernacles, to commemorate the event.

The Children of Israel put their trust in God completely. The price of their freedom was forty years of impermanence. Each night they would shelter in a different place, not knowing what the morrow held. This trial of trust and endurance purified their intent to enter the Promised Land as a nation, and anchored their faith in the Source to guide and support them.

Sukkot is ruled by the Angel of Permanence, who reassures us of God's enduring love and support. Many people strive mistakenly for external forms of security in their lives—the props of wealth, power, or social position—rather than cultivating the true permanence that can be found within us. If we nurture the lasting, essential part of our being, the immortal spark of Divinity at our core, we will be able withstand any challenge in life.

MEDITATION

Reflect on what is permanent within you, on what remains and endures. It is not your body, which ages, your emotions, which change like the wind, or your thoughts, which create change and give rise to new events. There is a place within you that never changes, is not born, and does not die. This is your Self. You build upon it each time you honor the Source within. This indelible part of you is called the I AM THAT I AM. When you address it you know that you are always connected to God.

ALL SAINTS' DAY

This feast day, presided over by the Angel of Good Deeds, venerates the selfless love and courage of all the Christian saints and martyrs.

November 1

Prayer

To the Angel of Good Deeds, be an example to us of our potential, so that we can be made whole by the kindness that comes from simple acts. These bless, enlighten, and serve our healing. Remind us to do good to others, be they friends, family, strangers, outcasts, or the lonely. We have the capacity for so much good. Help us to use it for the benefit of one another. Amen.

All Saints' Day, or All Hallows, is preceded by the night of Hallowe'en, when evil spirits roam about. By contrast, saints are supreme examples of the goodness and light within us. Good deeds help us to recognize this. They open our hearts to the understanding that we are all worthwhile, and add another dimension to our daily lives. We know that understanding and kindness can make a lasting impression. When we support and help each other from the goodness of our hearts, we become partners in perfecting Creation.

MEDITATION

Reflect on the opportunities you have to do good. A seemingly insignificant act can make a difference. It is a good deed when you let your spirit shine and offer someone a smile. Kind acts create good vibrations for you and for others.

ALL SOULS' DAY

This day of prayer is ruled by the Angel of the Divine Spirit. By cherishing our connection with the departed, we affirm the undying nature of our essential being.

Prayer

Beloved Angel of the Divine Spirit, remember our love for those who have departed this life, whose imprint leaves us better.
Help us to keep their spirit alive through the good we do. The Divine Spirit lives forever in every conscious act of loving.
We give thanks for all who have reached out to us with love and care.
Amen.

All Souls' Day commemorates the departed, the souls of ordinary good believers who are neither saints nor sinners. With the passing of time, the memory of those who have gone from our lives fades. We need to remind ourselves of the qualities we cherished in them. By remembering the spirits of our loved ones, old friends, or people who made a difference to us, we keep their spirits alive. Recalling their laughter, patience, or guidance is a way of reanimating those same qualities within ourselves.

We have all been blessed with people in our lives who left an indelible and positive mark on us. Taking this day to remember them with a candle, a reading from scripture, or a prayer, helps to purify their Divine spirit as well as our own. Love never dies. It stays in our souls forever.

MEDITATION

Reflect on the Divine spirits you have known in your life. They may have been intimate friends, family members, teachers, or people from whom you have learned courage, strength, laughter, humor, or love. Give thanks as you remember their essential spirits. You were blessed to experience them.

CHANUKKAH

The Jewish Festival of Lights is presided over by the Angel of Miracles. It commemorates the cleansing and rededication of the Temple after the expulsion of the pagan Greeks, and celebrates the miracle of the enduring flame. Chanukkah testifies to the triumph of truth and purity over falsehood and adversity.

Kislev 25–Tevet 2; in November–December

*C*hanukkah (Hebrew for "dedication") is the eight-day Jewish Festival of Lights. It celebrates the reconsecration of the Temple in Jerusalem by the victorious Maccabees in 165 B.C., after its desecration by the Hellenizing Greek ruler of Syria, Antiochus

Epiphanes. The Jews rededicated the Temple altar, and wished to rekindle the *menorah*, the seven-branched candelabrum that was kept burning at all times, but could find only a small jar of ritually pure olive oil for the purpose. Then a miracle occurred. The oil—enough for only one day—continued burning for eight days, the time needed to prepare new, pure oil.

This miracle is commemorated by the lighting of the eight-branched household Chanukkah lamp, one extra light being added on each successive night. The traditional interpretation of the miracle is that God enables the pure to give light well beyond its natural potential. The medieval mystics of the Kabbalah regarded the Chanukkah lights as a manifestation of the hidden light of the Messiah.

Chanukkah falls around midwinter, and is ruled by the Angel of Miracles. The miracle of lights thus suggests, on an inner level, that no matter how dark or tragic an event in our lives may be, our inner light is eternal, and can never die. Remembering this helps us to develop strength and clarity of purpose. We, too, are miracles of God's love, and the flame of the soul never dies.

MEDITATION

Reflect on the miracle of events that happen every day in your life. How much good comes to you in spite of the rash of negativity you may surround yourself with? How many people are healed, and brought alive by the miracle of love each day? Think about the common experiences of having your life, work, and everything in it functioning as it should. Open yourself to the everyday miracles that you take for granted.

Prayer

O, Angel of Miracles,
how many times have
you blessed us
with the coming of
your light,
which we have failed
to see.
Teach us to know the
gifts that you bring
from our Heavenly
Father,
and to recognize your
Divine Presence.
Miracles are an
everyday occurrence,
and yet we remain
oblivious to God's
power to heal the
world.
Teach us to be
grateful for the
countless miracles,
small and large, that
happen every day
to keep us
whole and well.
Amen.

41

ADVENT

The season of Advent, anticipating the coming of Christ, is presided over by the Angel of Expectation. It looks forward to the celebration of the birth of Jesus, and prepares the faithful for His second coming at the end of days. We prepare not just for the earthly life of Jesus, but for His continuing role as Redeemer over time.

The Sunday nearest to November 30 in the West; November 15 in the East

In most branches of Christianity, the Christian year starts on Advent Sunday, the fourth Sunday before Christmas. The following weeks, leading up to Christmas, are the season of Advent. The Latin word

adventus means "coming" or "arrival," and this is a time of spiritual preparation, not only for the coming of the Light of Christ at the beginning of the Christian era, but also for His return at the end of days.

In the Roman Catholic Church, Advent is observed with contemplation, abstinence, and austerities. Advent candles are lit, and in many Christian traditions, Nativity plays are performed.

This festival, in the deepening winter, is ruled by the Angel of Expectation. The anticipation of Christmas is a reminder to direct our thoughts to the return of the Light, symbolized by the birth of the Christ Child. We mark the days preceding this event until we, too, are reborn in the holy light of inner purity.

Advent is a time for reflection, for turning to our inner light and finding the selfless love for humanity that is celebrated universally at Christmas. Our thoughts turn to showing our love with gifts, and to finding ways to ease the pain and suffering of those in need. We celebrate the innocence and purity of the holy child living in every heart during this season.

MEDITATION

Reflect on the time when you were a child and had prepared a long list of the presents you wanted for Christmas. Did you get what you had hoped for? Now open your heart to the needs of others who don't even dare to expect Christmas to be better than the other days of the year. Let Advent remind you that this is a time to act consciously to bring more light into the world, to let your sense of goodness and generosity shine.

Prayer

*O, Angel of
Expectation,
you ask us to honor
the coming of the
Light,
and to prepare our
souls for the richness
of giving.
Help us to accept
with joy the goodness
that this season
brings.
Remember the
innocence in all of us.
Help us to temper our
desires,
and bring to our
awareness ways in
which we can each
make a difference
in the expansion of
the Christ light in a
dark world.
Amen.*

43

CHRISTMAS

December 25

The Birthday of Christ, the creator incarnate, is one of the most joyful days in the Christian year. Presided over by the Angel of Divine Light, it celebrates the moment when the Word became Flesh, and God came into the world as a pure and innocent child in order to redeem us with His infinite love.

*C*hristmas celebrates the birth of Jesus Christ, two thousand years ago. One of the holiest days in the Christian year, it is the pivotal point of the belief that Jesus was God incarnate, a man filled with the essential nature of God. The gift of this Divine child, the Light of the World, who would experience human suffering, and conquer sin and death, is the measure of God's great self-sacrificing love. He entered the world in order to save it.

The date for the observance of Christmas reflects the pagan past. Rome's winter solstice feast of the Birth of the Unconquered Sun, on December 25, was transmuted by the fathers of the early Church to celebrate the coming of the "Sun of Righteousness."

At Christmas the Divine Light entered the world in human form to awaken the hearts and spirits of men. This joyful miracle demonstrates the greatness of God's love. Together with the Angel of Divine Light, we rejoice in the birth of hope for eternal life and in the promise of fulfillment of our highest desires.

MEDITATION

Reflect on the Holy Child, born in humble circumstances to trusting parents. In a world of strife, this child became a living example to humanity of the fulfillment of spiritual potential. God gave His son to heal the world. Does not every child have Divine potential to do the same? Seek the child within yourself, the pure and innocent part of you that needs love, care, and respect, and you will connect with the Divine Light within.

44

Prayer

*Most precious Angel
of Divine Light,
illuminate our spirits
and purify our
hearts.
Help us to accept and
to cherish the gift of
eternal life that you
offer.
Your presence opens
the door to God's
light, which we
welcome gladly.
Heal us, so that we
may contribute
to the healing
of this world.
Amen.*

Behold I bring you good tidings of great joy

A HAPPY CHRISTMAS

CANDLEMAS

February 2

The festival of Candlemas, or the Presentation of the Lord, is presided over by the Angel of Honor. The recognition and veneration of the Christ Child as the Messiah by Simeon is a call to honor all manifestations of the Divine Light, in the world, and within ourselves.

*W*hen, as was the custom, Joseph and Mary took the infant Jesus to the Temple in Jerusalem to be dedicated to the Lord, and to complete Mary's purification rites, he was recognized by Simeon and the prophetess Anna as the promised Messiah. Candlemas, the traditional English name for the festival celebrating their recognition of His divinity, refers to the candlelight procession before Mass honoring the entry of the True Light into the world.

The Divine Light lives within each person. It is the greater glory of our true nature, which embraces integrity, dignity, and a passion for life. When we kindle our inner light at Candlemas, we honor and celebrate the Self. This reminds us to stay true to our spiritual quest, to know, love, and respect who we are at source, and to stand up for what we believe to be right.

In celebrating this day, we honor all those who fulfill a higher purpose, or who were martyred, imprisoned, or died for their principles. Honoring the Divine light of Self means standing up for what we believe to be right, and defending what we know to be true.

MEDITATION

Reflect on honor, on your association with honorable causes and with people who have lived their lives honorably. Have you been faced with the need to make choices for your highest good? Knowing what is honorable and worthwhile makes a difference to the way you respond to people and handle challenging situations in your life. You know that, given a choice between doing right or wrong, you would always choose the right and honorable path.

Prayer

O, Angel of Honor, bless us
with the awareness that you bring
in these dark times.
Illuminate our path so that our spirit
can shine outward
toward the higher road.
Help us to stand firm for the principles
we know to be true,
and enable us to overcome fear
in times of peril.
Guide us on our way home
to the Light within, and, above all,
help us to honor our spirit.
Amen.

YOM HASHOAH

Holocaust Day is presided over by the Angel of Remembrance. The martyrdom of Jewry by the Nazis poses difficult questions about human nature and Divine providence. We remind ourselves of the full spectrum of human potential for good and evil, and reaffirm the necessity for wisdom, love, and compassion in our lives.

Nisan 27; in April

This Jewish holy day commemorates the genocide perpetrated by the Nazis against the Jews of Europe during the Second World War. The term "holocaust" refers to their highly organized campaign of mass killing, the like of which the world had never seen. The date of this painful day of remembrance changes within the Hebrew calendar to accord with April 19, the day in 1943 when the Jews of the Warsaw Ghetto rose up in revolt against the fate decreed for them.

What can we make of such evil as the Holocaust? How can we reconcile man's inhumanity to man with a belief in a benevolent Creator? Such wholesale perversion of our highest principles is a denial of the Godhead within us. It is the abyss that we fall into when we cut ourselves off from the spark of divinity. True self-knowledge must take into account the evidence of human depravity. We must never forget what we are capable of. With this in mind, we can turn to our inner light with deeper understanding.

On this solemn and cathartic day, we think of the unimaginable human suffering, of the loss of life and potential brought about by hatred and ignorance. We need to confront the events of the past with understanding, so that we can live more fully in the present and be reconciled to the world. This day is thus dedicated to survival, and to the affirmation of life. To remain bitter over what cannot be changed is to spoil the precious life we have now. We are helped by remembering the joy that people have brought into our lives, the kindness we have experienced, and the love we have shared. To understand the human condition is to set our spirit free to find new life, new love, new joy.

Prayer

Blessed Angel of Remembrance,
hold up a candle to the past to remind us of
our need to understand the wellsprings
of human behavior.
Teach us to value love, kindness, and joy,
while the memory of goodness stays in our
soul, and help us to recover from our wounds.
Heal our hearts, and enable us to live
consciously in the present, sharing fully in
this special gift of life.
Amen.

MEDITATION

Release negative memories of the past
by forgiving the hurt done to you. Say
goodbye to old attachments that limit
the gift of the present and steal
precious moments of life from you.
Let go the memory of incidents that
aggravate your sense of loss and
separation. The more fully you can
bring yourself into the present, letting
the past rest in peace, the more you will
find understanding and reconciliation.
This is the pathway to healing. The
choice to live in the now is yours.

The Higher Principles

Angels are the agents of the Higher Principles, the unchanging laws that govern creation. These are expressed through the Shekhinah, Jesus, and the Virgin Mary, and relate to our capacity to love, to accept ourselves fully, and to embrace life.

Within heaven there is a three-tiered hierarchy, ascending by degrees of love and awareness, and within each realm there are three categories of angels. The highest level, the Heaven of Form, contains the love, protection, and guidance of the Archangels, our personal Guardian Angels, and the Angel Princes who rule specific geographic locations.

The Heaven of Creation is blessed with the tender, merciful energies of the Powers, Virtues, and Dominions. These angels affect our spiritual development directly. They bring peace and harmony to our lives. They help us to accept ourselves, to open our hearts to God's love, to reconcile ourselves to loss, and to forgive.

The Heaven of Paradise contains the glory and power of the Seraphim, the Cherubim, and the Thrones, who are the angels of love, wisdom, and glory.

Reigning above the heavenly host is the spirit of the Shekhinah, the feminine face of the Divine, through whom all creation is made manifest. The heavenly realm interacts with the physical world, and the two become one, in the incarnation of Jesus Christ. The Higher Principles thus find expression in spirit and in flesh. The lives of Jesus and Mary show God working directly in the world, and are the fulfillment of our highest desire. Their example brings the love and guidance of the angels into our everyday reality to help us realize our highest good.

THE SHEKHINAH, BRIDE OF THE LORD

In Judaism, the manifestation of the Divine Presence in human life takes the form of a created being of light called the Shekhinah. Meaning literally "indwelling," this is the feminine aspect of God that brings peace and blessing to the home. In biblical times it referred to the glory emanating from the Source. The Shekhinah was then seen as a heavenly messenger, and later as the Holy Ghost. In the Kabbalah, she is the mystical Bride of the Lord, who channels grace to the lower worlds. She is also the Sabbath Bride, who blesses the union of man and wife, because the restoration of the flawed world through love is the fulfillment of God's purpose.

Because we contain the Divine spark within us, our actions resonate throughout creation. By virtuous deeds we help to unite the Shekhinah with the Godhead, and to elevate ourselves to a higher spiritual plane. In opening our hearts to the joy and comfort that she brings, we celebrate life, and integrate our male and female sides into a single harmonious whole.

MEDITATION

Reflect on the passive and receptive side of your own nature. Allow yourself to be open to receive the goodness of the universe, and to express your gratitude with gentleness and kindness. In a world committed to a strong, outgoing, male energy, learn to embrace the female aspect of your own spirit. This quality will bring more balance, wholeness, and harmony into your life.

Prayer

*Beloved Shekhinah,
remind us of the
receptive side of God,
where your beauty
and presence soothe,
nurture, and heal our
hearts.
We pray for the
ability to accept the
soft and gentle
aspects of our nature
as essential parts of
who we are.
Help us to mirror the
female side of our
Creator with
gratitude, and so
become whole.
Amen.*

JESUS CHRIST, LORD OF HEAVEN AND EARTH

Beloved Jesus, Lord God,
we turn our hearts and minds to you, to feel your power within us.
Help us to find the love and healing that you represent within ourselves.
Teach us to know you through our higher minds, so that we may grow in grace and humility,
and live in the spirit of perfection for which you are the template.
Help us to accept your unconditional love, which frees us from inner strife.
Receive us, parent us, and help us to reach our fullest potential.
Accept our prayers of thanksgiving,
and let us become that which we are meant to be.
Amen.

Jesus came to fulfill human aspirations and to embody the highest of universal principles, that of unconditional love. He is the Word made flesh. He was born, lived, and died so that the human spirit could evolve, and mankind be raised to a higher level of spiritual awareness. His incarnation and crucifixion redeem us from sin and restore us to communion with God; we have been liberated from darkness by the light of His love.

Jesus is a model of perfection to which the human spirit can aspire. Knowing that His spirit lives within us, and recognizing it as the Source of all goodness, light, and joy, enables us to develop into whole rather than fragmented beings. By aligning ourselves with the highest principle, we give our lives a clear foundation.

The best, most noble, and wholesome part of ourselves, which is the Christ light within us, is what leads us to safety when we are in danger of losing our way in life. This is the greater awareness to whom we pray for guidance, protection, and sustenance. We ask to be lifted up through His love and healing.

When we allow the Christ light to shine within us, we attain those qualities that Jesus embodies. He lives in that part of us which is eternal. Here, on this earthly plane, we evolve toward a higher spirituality through the Divine principle within us.

Christ totally supports us in our tasks of learning. He is the supreme teacher and comforter, whose presence is our hope and refuge. We offer Him our thanks, and release our fears and doubts as we put our trust in the way before us.

Turning to the Christ light takes humility, and a belief that God gave His son for our deepest growth and development. Christ is the embodiment of perfection, wholeness, and the power of God to work in us. We become spiritual beings when we accept the seed of perfection that He represents within us.

MEDITATION

Find the place where Christ lives within you. You may look within your higher mind, and in your heart. You do not need to seek far; you have only to take the time to look within. Where the Christ light shines are the words "I AM THAT I AM," first revealed to Moses in the burning bush. Know this to be the essence of your Self.

THE BLESSED VIRGIN MARY, MOTHER OF GOD

*Blessed and Beloved
Mother of us all,
you surrendered to
the will of God to
bear the fruit of our
salvation.
You accepted a higher
will than your own so
that all humanity
could be raised up.
We ask for healing
through your
intercession.
Please accept our
humble plea for
grace, love, and
courage.
Amen.*

The Blessed Virgin Mary, mother of Christ, is our link with the eternal feminine principle within us. She is the embodiment of truth, love, and sacrifice. In the Roman Catholic Church, she is the first of all the Saints, honored as the woman destined to be the pure vessel through which the Christ light entered the world.

Mary obtains grace for us by her maternal intercession. She is the channel to the Divine through which we pass as we purify our hearts. Her litany describes her as Queen of Angels, Mother of God, Mother Inviolate, Tower of Ivory, House of Gold, Mystical Rose, and Gate of Heaven.

We honor Mary as the Great Mother archetype. She is the goddess of fertility, healing, and love, the magical feminine to which we all aspire. She is the source of miraculous cures, who appears in moments of darkness to the innocent and pure of heart, bringing the hope and comfort of the word of God. Her shrines around the world attract multitudes of pilgrims.

MEDITATION

Reflect on aspects of motherhood that you cherish, such as mother most lovable, mother of good counsel, or mother of divine grace. Hold the spirit of the Holy Mother in your mind. Sense the goodness, purity, and love deep within you. Recall that Mary witnessed her son's death and chose, again, to put her faith and trust in God. Despite her grief, she was able to release Him into His father's keeping. Awareness of this act of love can open your heart to great healing.

Spring

Spring marks new beginnings and signifies rebirth. Light returns to the world and all life is renewed.

The vernal equinox, about March 21, is ruled by the Archangel Raphael, who brings healing to the world.

The vernal equinox is the most auspicious date of the year. This is the halfway point between winter and summer, when the sun crosses the plane of the equator on its journey toward us, making day and night of equal length. As the days lengthen, the earth warms up and new life emerges everywhere, assuring us that the sun's light-giving power is again within our grasp. We know that once our hemisphere has crossed into the light we will have time for beauty, play, and pleasure. Life will be easier, both physically and spiritually.

At this juncture the energy forces of the earth are balanced. Darkness and light are in harmony. This is an excellent time to release the old and embrace the new. We shut the doors on the cold, dark days of winter and look forward to the warmth and ease of light-filled days and the return of the life force flowing in us.

Major religious holidays fall within weeks of the vernal equinox. Easter and Passover are both calculated by the night of the first full moon after this day, followed by Pentecost and Shavuot. Underpinning the traditional theological significance of these festivals is the primal knowledge of the earth's cycle.

At this time we thank God for the healing that has redeemed us from the difficulties in our lives. We welcome another cycle of life that provides our spirits with wholesome opportunities for regeneration, growth, and healing.

MEDITATION

Sit quietly and breathe gently, bringing your awareness within yourself. Feel yourself coming into contact with Raphael, the envoy of God's healing light. Reflect on what healing would be like for you, and how you would know that it had occurred in your life. Imagine this energy being directed to you. You can draw it into yourself, to bring you the healing and joy you need. Be open to the power of God, manifested as good health.

Prayer

*O, beloved Raphael,
we give thanks for
our health and
well-being.
With deep gratitude
we receive your
blessings
of God's love,
manifested in
joyful health.
We rejoice in the
return of our life force
by the grace of your
healing love.
Please protect all that
is vital and living
in each of us.
Restore our spirit to a
state of grace,
and purify our hearts
to receive the bounty
of joy, love, and
healing that God
provides.
Amen.*

The Archangel Raphael

Raphael brings us the regenerative life force of God. His name means "God is healing." He journeys on the wings of the wind and acts as the bearer of God's love to mankind. His healing can come in the form of knowledge or of energy that restores us to wholeness. He is thought to wear a tablet engraved with God's name, and his symbol is a serpent. Raphael is one of the seven holy angels who sit at the throne of God. He rules over the second level of heaven. He is first seen in the Book of Tobit, when he cures Tobit of his blindness with a salve of ash from the burnt bladder of a fish. For this reason he is often shown carrying a fish. In the Book of Enoch he is one of "the Watchers," and one who is set over the diseases and wounds of humanity. According to *The Zohar* he heals the earth and furnishes an abode for man. He is the Guardian of the Tree of Life in the Garden of Eden, and holds a medical book describing all the healing substances God has given to mankind. He is also known as the Angel of the Sun, and as the Angel of Science and Knowledge.

We turn to Raphael when we are ill at any level. His gifts come in many forms, including herbs, plants, and the knowledge of color. He encourages us to look within, and to mend any sense of separation from the Source, the causal factor in all disease. He blesses healers, doctors, nurses, and all who offer their talents and gifts in the art of healing.

	Aries March 21–April 20	Taurus April 21–May 20	Gemini May 21–June 21
ELEMENT	Fire	Earth	Air
COLOR	Red	Red-orange	Orange
RULING PLANET	Mars	Venus	Mercury
PART OF BODY	The head and the face	The neck and the throat	The arms and the shoulders
ANGEL	*The Angel of Renewal*	*The Angel of Earthly Desires*	*The Angel of Inspiration*
FESTIVALS	EASTER *The Angel of Resurrection* PASSOVER *The Angel of Redemption*		PENTECOST *The Angel of Gratitude* SHAVUOT *The Angel of Strength*

ANGEL OF THE WEEK

	Aries	Taurus	Gemini
WEEK 1	*The Angel of Rebirth*	*The Angel of Vitality*	*The Angel of Transformation*
WEEK 2	*The Angel of Faith*	*The Angel of Abundance*	*The Angel of Celebration*
WEEK 3	*The Angel of Hope*	*The Angel of Beauty*	*The Angel of Joy*
WEEK 4	*The Angel of Trust*	*The Angel of Wisdom*	*The Angel of Recreation*

Aries

ELEMENT: *Fire*

COLOR: *Red*

RULING PLANET: *Mars*

FESTIVALS: *Easter
Passover*

ANGEL: *The Angel of
Renewal*

Prayer

*Dearest Angel of Renewal,
please guide us to renew our focus
and commitment to life.
Help us to purge the doubts, fears,
and bad habits that arrest our
growth.
Renew that part of us which is
weak and afraid.
We pray for renewed energy in our
bodies, minds, and spirits,
so that we can complete our tasks
and satisfy our longing for
wholeness.
We give thanks for renewed vigor.
Amen.*

The Angel of Renewal corresponds to the first sign of the zodiac, Aries, when new life emerges and all living things are quickened. Aries signifies the awakening of vitality, which has been dormant within the earth during the winter months. The power of fire, symbolized by the fiery planet Mars, and the intensity of the emerging life force flood our spirits with natural energy, and we feel the strength of God entering creation and recharging us for the year ahead.

At this time of year life is rich in self-expression, and recreates itself in endless forms of unfolding patterns. The impact of this angel is felt by all who experience renewed life coursing through their veins. The Angel of Renewal confirms our right to life, and helps us to affirm our intention to live in joy and peace. He offers us the best possibilities for reestablishing our lives on a healthy foundation, and helps us to find hope and trust in the inherent goodness of life.

MEDITATION

Feel your heart expand and contract with each breath that you take. Let it soften and ease as you affirm life. As you do this, be conscious that you are opening up to your life force with each breath. This is how you experience renewal at all levels.

As you feel this happen, ask yourself where you need to renew your commitment to life, to be the best that you can be. Renewal comes when you affirm your desire to accept life on its terms.

Angels of the week

The green shoots of spring affirm the possibility of spiritual renewal.

WEEK ONE

THE ANGEL OF REBIRTH

Prayer

Rebirth is the central theme of spring, when the emerging beauty and freshness of new life is juxtaposed with our awareness that life is eternal and that our spirit never dies. This knowledge comes from the Source within us, where life is in a perpetual state of rebirth. As we surrender our ego to our higher self, we release old and rigid parts of ourselves that fail to serve our highest good. At each stage of this surrender a new awareness of life emerges, and we are reborn into the continuous flow of grace that comes with growth and change. As each layer of our old self is shed, our essential being emerges in a truer likeness of the Divine. In our spiritual rebirth we affirm love, life, and the glory of God as we find new ways to share our inner light with those around us.

O, Angel of Rebirth,
awaken us to the
awareness
that life is eternally
reborn,
and that our soul's
expression is itself the
elixir of life.
We celebrate and
accept ourselves at
each stage
of life.
Show us what is
permanent,
and what remains
unchanged.
Let us be aware of the
living spirit
within,
and that we emerge
reborn
in each cycle of life.
Amen.

MEDITATION

Be aware of what feels old, tired, and unyielding in you. As you breathe gently, visualize these parts of yourself softening, relaxing, and melting. Look within to examine the places that are fixed, or resistant to change. Choose to release the knots of tension and rigid patterns of thought compelling you always to be right, and allow the joy of rebirth to expand and fill your spirit.

Rebirth comes to us when we let go of the old, implacable ideas about ourselves and life in general, and make room for the new to come to us.

Faith can move mountains, heal the sick and realize the impossible.

WEEK TWO

THE ANGEL OF FAITH

Prayer

*O, Angel of Faith, show us belief in the goodness of life, and understanding that the universe is benign.
When we are lost, help us to find faith and to live close to the spirit.
Renew our faith in the intrinsic goodness of life, and in our ability to fulfill our purpose as God envisages it.
Amen.*

As we move into spring, and the earth awakens from her winter slumber, weather patterns can be volatile. In our inner world, too, our renewed commitment to life may face challenges that can blow us off course. We need faith to keep on track with our highest intentions in changing conditions. A life rich in faith looks beyond doubt and cynicism. With faith in the intrinsic goodness of life, we cultivate awareness of the larger picture that enables us to transcend difficult situations.

MEDITATION

Reflect on something you wish to realize now. This can involve your life, your work, or your relationships. Ask yourself if you have faith in the positive results that you desire. You may not know how things will transpire to bring about your wishes, but having faith that it will happen is all you need. Faith in life will save you time, energy, and worry. It will give you the inner assurance that life is working for your good, and create a virtuous circle leading to positive outcomes.

Hope is part of a healthy attitude to life. It can open doors.

WEEK THREE

THE ANGEL OF HOPE

Hope springs eternal in the soul. It is part of the human condition to hope for goodness and light to triumph. This is because we know that we are eternally connected to the power of good through the presence of God. We remain hopeful in the face of the most forbidding circumstances, and even though things may not turn out as we wish. Hope helps us to get through painful or difficult times. Hope is that aspect of human nature that comes from the heart. It is part of our desire for the good to unfold, and is rooted in the deepest memory of love, goodness, and joy. It is the optimism born of faith in a benevolent and meaningful creation. Cultivate hope in the good as you set yourself new goals in life. It will open the doors of opportunity for good to come to you.

Prayer

*Beloved Angel of Hope,
spring eternal in our hearts
so that we can envisage the best unfolding of events.
Nurture this quality arising from the purity of our hearts.
Help us to find our spirit,
beyond the tides of external reality,
in the core of our soul where hope lives.
Let us always hope for the best
for ourselves
and for those we hold dear.
Amen.*

MEDITATION

Let your mind wander to the past, to when you were a small child. Can you remember the times you hoped for something so badly that you felt your heart would break if it didn't happen? Can you remember hoping, even against hope itself, that you would win, be chosen, find a friend, be loved, cared for, or not punished for something you regretted doing?

Now extract the energy from the situation that you remember, and revive that quality of hope in your mind. Find that pure place within yourself where hope wins, and the results you longed for can be achieved. Hope is your focused intention for the good to manifest itself in your life.

Angels of the week

Placing our trust in life is a serene affirmation of its positive nature.

WEEK FOUR

THE ANGEL OF TRUST

Trust underpins our hope and faith. It stems from our experience of the Divine power within us, and from the unshakable knowledge that life supports us. Trust is implicit in our deeper awareness that life is good, and that we are part of a greater whole, always connected, always included. It is this assurance that sustains us when life appears painful or difficult, and when the way ahead is not clear. We trust in life to support us in our process of growth and development. Even though we may not appreciate what is happening, or fully understand the risks involved, it does mean that in our hearts we know that all will be well, no matter how difficult things may seem.

We develop our trust in God to guide and protect us, and to bring us peace, by being willing to relinquish control over our lives. We turn our fears, doubts, and anxieties over to Him in prayer, in the belief that He will provide our highest good and greatest joy. Prayer reinforces our connection with God, and the knowledge that we are in His care. We trust in ourselves, we trust in the process of life to unfold as it should, and we trust in the Almighty to lead us to a safe haven.

Prayer

Blessed Angel of Trust,
ignite the spark of trust in God's
abiding love for us.
Let it open doors to goodness and joy.
Let us trust that good will manifest itself
in every way in our lives.
Help us to trust in the Holy Spirit,
and to know that whatever unfolds
is meant to be.
Amen.

MEDITATION

To trust that pleasure will last, and that love will abide, are positive beliefs that mirror the strongest life principles we hold. Trust comes from the depths of your being. Breathe into your heart and find the jewel of trust at its center. As you touch this place, affirm your trust in life.

Affirmation is confirming what is positive, whole, and good in your life. It is staying attuned to the positive, even amid doubt and fear. Testify to your trust in the eternal verities, in the presence of the Divine acting in your life, and in your highest good. Your affirmation will open doors.

Taurus

ELEMENT: *Earth*

COLOR: *Red-orange*

RULING PLANET: *Venus*

ANGEL: *The Angel of Earthly Desires*

Taurus is an earth sign grounded in the pleasures of life, and ruling a season of glorious colors and verdant beauty. This is spring at its best, when new growth and emergent energy are fully established. Burgeoning life awakens our creative urge and the need to express ourselves in many ways. It is a time to acknowledge the depths of our desires.

This is a productive time for regeneration, stability, and a sense of well-being. Now is the moment to affirm relationships, to

Prayer

Dear Angel of Earthly Desires,
help us to appreciate
all that we have,
and teach us the appropriate
measure of material things.
Open our eyes to the wealth and
riches we possess, both in our inner
life and in the outer world.
We pray for the resources we need to
live in the way we enjoy,
and we are thankful for our ability
to manifest the goodness we desire.
Help us to learn to be comfortable
with abundance.
Amen.

look at our homes and workplaces and think of fresh paint, new colors and furnishings, or to make decisions about our physical health. It is a time to enjoy material possessions, when we give ourselves the things and experiences that provide pleasure and delight, translating our desires into reality. The Angel of Earthly Desires presides over this season, helping us to appreciate and accept abundance as part of our birthright, and to acknowledge the power of creation that we have at our fingertips.

MEDITATION

Think of all the people who bring delight into your life. You may conjure up your personal relationship with a significant other; or a group of friends who share your vision of life.

You might like to think about family members, pets, or associates whom you love and appreciate.

Imagine all these people gathered around you. See them acknowledging you, caring for your happiness and welfare. Enjoy feeling good about yourself, and know that you have enough of the love, money, and attention that you deserve. Trust and accept that the goodness you long for will come to you.

Angels of the week

Abundant energy is yours when you love what you do and do what you love.

WEEK ONE

THE ANGEL OF VITALITY

This is the season when life's energy runs high, and we want to share in its natural abundance. We long to have enough energy to accomplish all the things we want to do. Our vitality is the summation of our physical well-being, our emotional state, and our creativity. Thus the more we channel our activities into things that are heartfelt, that honor our sense of self, and that allow our inner light to shine, the greater our physical vitality becomes.

In order to have the vitality we want, we need to identify personal attitudes that limit our well-being, such as doubt and fear. Nothing depletes the life force faster than negative thoughts. They sap our natural vitality and drain away our goodness. We may need to take time to reevaluate what we do with our life energy, possibly to consider a period of rest and regeneration, a complete break from the people and places of our everyday lives. The more we honor our inner self and listen to what is needed in terms of rest, regeneration, and activity, the greater our vitality will be, and the longer we will be able to do the things we love.

Prayer

*Dearest Angel of Vitality,
help us to use our energy wisely,
and to conserve it for what is
healthy and wholesome.
Help us to live a positive and
useful life, and give us energy to do
the things we love.
Teach us the difference between
what feels good and
what is really good for us,
so that we use our energy to rightful purpose,
and have an abundance of it
to do God's work.
Amen.*

MEDITATION

Visualize yourself having all the energy you need to do the things you enjoy. This may be having a good time with friends and family; it might be an activity like swimming, sailing, skiing, or cycling, or just relaxing with a good book under an umbrella. Know that you feel good and love what you are doing. Accept that abundant energy is yours when you love what you do and can put your whole heart into it.

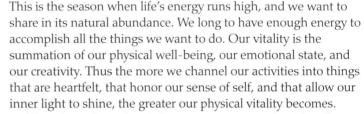

Positive attitudes will generate a virtuous circle of fulfillment.

THE ANGEL OF ABUNDANCE

Prayer

Beloved Angel of Abundance, open our eyes to see how rich and prosperous we truly are. Open our hearts to celebrate in joyous gratitude the treasures we possess. Teach us to value our gifts, conserve our resources, and nourish our reserves on the inner and outer planes of existence. Amen.

Our sense of abundance arises from our experience of the goodness of the universe. When we claim our highest good and greatest joy, the world appears to be miraculously responsive. We experience being and having enough. With every affirmation, our energy generates more good things in our lives.

We can choose to experience the world as empty, lacking, and failing to provide what we want in terms of love or money, or we can see it as rich, prosperous, and inviting us to participate in its goodness. It is up to us to decide whether the proverbial glass is "half empty" or "half full," for it is not what we have that gives us a feeling of insufficiency or wealth, but rather our attitude to what we have, what we do, and who we are.

The riches we already have, whether material or spiritual, are enough for us to know that life is bountiful. Gratitude for the blessings that life brings will make our lives meaningful, happy, and abundant.

MEDITATION

Let go of any ideas you have about yourself that reflect an attitude of insufficiency or inadequacy.

Affirm that you are deeply thankful for all that you have in your life. Let your gratitude cover your material possessions, your emotional ties, your spiritual insights and values, and your ever-present connection with God. Be grateful for the goodness that fills your life. You are, in fact, much richer than you think.

THE ANGEL OF BEAUTY

Beauty is the reflection of who we are; it is not achieved.

When we connect with our true Self, we find that beauty is an innate quality. As we begin to know our worth and to value ourselves, we come to accept beauty as part of our birthright. We actually grow more beautiful as we become more truly ourselves.

Real beauty does not depend on time, age, shape, wealth, race, or size. It transcends form. It is a quality issuing directly from our essence, which expands as we realign ourselves with our core. Beauty is who we are.

Beauty is present in all living forms. When something is beautiful it is expressing the truth of its being. Whether it is a person whom we experience as beautiful, an animal whose grace or majesty we admire, or a flower that captures our senses, the presence of beauty resonates within us, and we are captivated. We recognize it from the place within ourselves where beauty resides as part of our own Divine essence.

Human beauty is as much a part of every person as a soul. It is not conditional on fashion, trends, or the acceptance of other people. It is an inner quality that longs to be nurtured, revealed, and expressed. It is a function of our spirit shining out into the world. This radiance emanating from the center of our being expresses itself to other people with a smile, a warm-hearted gesture, or goodness of spirit. It connects us by virtue of its ability to resonate within us. It reminds us of the unity of life, and of its transience. We find beauty in a flower that will wilt tomorrow, a butterfly that may live only a few days, or a carefree child who will grow up into a responsible adult.

Outer beauty teaches us to enjoy it in the moment. Inner beauty stays in the soul forever. Whether or not our spiritual beauty finds expression in the world depends largely on our desire to let our inner light shine. To open the window on our beauty we need to overcome self-consciousness. We can call on the Angel of Beauty and ask to be connected to what is permanently beautiful within us. Our spirits are a reflection of that inner light that is eternally brilliant. In each life, in every experience, the opportunity is given to us to let that beauty realize its potential.

Prayer

Beloved Angel of Beauty,
let us truly see ourselves as you
see us, and know our radiance
to be a gift from God.
When others see us, let them
experience our beauty, and
let that glow illuminate their
minds and warm their hearts.
Let our beauty invite,
heal, and soothe.
Amen.

MEDITATION

Visualize yourself looking and feeling beautiful. Try to hold this image in your mind's eye. See yourself smiling, relaxed, happy, and at peace. Feel your inner beauty radiating out to those around you. Allow yourself to be the shining light in the world that you know you are. This light is your beauty. Smile, relax, feel happy, and be at peace with yourself and the world.

Wisdom in judgment springs from the knowledge of God's love.

WEEK FOUR

THE ANGEL OF WISDOM

Prayer

*Blessed Angel of Wisdom,
guide us in developing
this most precious gift.
Let our wisdom be a beacon to
lead us through the perils
of human activity.
Teach us wisdom in all situations.
Give our thoughts clarity, our hearts
compassion, and our actions
nobility.
Remind us how dependent
our spirits are on God's knowing
and loving wisdom to guide us on the
pathways of love and healing.
Amen.*

The Bible tells us that wisdom is more valuable than gold. Without it, we lack a spiritual operating principle to guide us to a higher level of awareness. Unable to learn from our experiences, we are condemned to repeat our mistakes, and fail to grow to the full measure of our capabilities. We gain wisdom from painful as well as positive experiences. It enables us to measure ourselves and others, it tempers our behavior, inhibits our impulses, and shows us how to negotiate the complexities of human relationships.

In seeking wisdom, we cultivate understanding, forgiveness, and compassion—qualities that can release us from past negativity and enable us to live in the present, which is where potential is realized and goodness is achieved. Wisdom is the gift of maturity, experience, and faith in the higher principle of God's love, which sees us through difficulties and challenges.

MEDITATION

Ask your Higher Self, that part of the Divine in you, to reveal to you your essential wisdom about the current situation in your life. See the wisdom of making the necessary changes that will open doors to freedom, greater self-expression, and deeper feelings of happiness.

Ask your Higher Self for wisdom regarding your path in life, to know what will help you on your way. Seek the wisdom, when empowered, to be responsible and compassionate. After all, we are all called to seek wisdom in our life. As surely as you look for it, it will appear to you. Wisdom is a gift of the Self to the self.

Gemini

ELEMENT: *Air*

COLOR: *Orange*

RULING PLANET: *Mercury*

FESTIVALS: *Pentecost*
Shavuot

ANGELS: *The Angel of*
Inspiration

Gemini is an air sign that influences ideas, thoughts, and concepts. It rules a time of the year when there is so much beauty and new life in nature that our thoughts turn naturally to creation. We cannot see all this beauty without some thought of the Source. This season has traditionally inspired artists to create, and in their own small way to imitate, God. The Angel of Inspiration comes to us when we are open to this sense of wonder. He taps us on the shoulder and insists that we express our own creativity. He is the muse of all creative minds and spirits.

Gemini embraces the dual nature of life. We are both earthly beings with Divine spirit, and Spirit made as man. The heavenly Twins represent this duality, reminding us that we are both spirit and flesh. This is particularly evident in early summer, when we see nature flourishing, and we translate our awareness of this into ideas and creativity. With maturity we are better able to hold these different realities in our grasp. In our youth, the pull is more to the physical. As we grow older, the realm of the spirit predominates. At the mid-point of our lives we are able to incorporate both aspects into our consciousness. Both our participation in, and our abstraction of, nature express this uniquely human capacity to live simultaneously in heaven and on earth.

MEDITATION

You can nurture the channels of inspiration in different ways— by listening to the stately movement of baroque music, painting or drawing with your non-dominant hand, lying on your back and looking at the clouds, or being alone in nature. Inspiration comes when we make the effort to invite it to us. It often comes when we are happy and at peace with ourselves. Listening to the vibrancy and harmony of the angelic realms has inspired the greatest minds in art and science.

Prayer

*O, Angel of
Inspiration,
touch our minds with
waves of heavenly
delight and show us
the realm of
possibilities, where
we can play in the
fields of the Lord.
Thank you for
whispering in our
ears, opening our
eyes, and
generating your
life-affirming creative
principle within
our minds.
Inspire us to love
more and to bring
healing with
all our efforts.
Amen.*

Prayer

Dear Angel of Transformation,
open our hearts to the truth
of who we are.
Let us readily accept
the power and grace within us.
Transform our minds to realize
that God dwells within us.
Allow our spiritual insights
to protect, fortify, and
guide us along our path.
Amen.

MEDITATION

Reflect on a part of your personality that you would like to transform. It may be fear, doubt, cynicism, detachment, or entanglement. When you have defined this aspect of yourself, think about what you would like to replace it with. For instance, if you are fearful of change, you may wish to develop confidence and resilience. If you are cynical, you may wish to become more accepting and open. Energy does not exist in a vacuum, and so when we let go of something negative we need to replace it with something positive that serves us well.

Transformation is the process of growth toward enlightenment.

WEEK ONE

THE ANGEL OF TRANSFORMATION

At this time of year we can easily avail ourselves of the beauty of nature. It is a wonderful time for a holiday, or for visiting natural beauty spots and feeling the earth's energy work upon us. This resonance with nature heightens our personal transformation, and we perceive our part in God's plan with greater clarity and more positive intent.

Transformation is our changing, growing awareness of that which is permanent and unchanging within us, our divinity, or spirit. We can delve into the inner realm of transformation by releasing attachment to loss, fear, or doubt, allowing our inner light to shine brightly, and by placing our small local self in the greater expanded arena of the higher Self, where God's Holy Spirit illuminates our being. This awareness transforms our thoughts and actions, and the enlightened way we behave transforms our relations with the people around us.

Transformation creates joy, healing, and unity. It is life-affirming on every level, inner and outer, and reflects our deepest awareness of Self. Take advantage of these portal days to let the light of transformation shine brightly within you. Use this time to become more aware of who you truly are, and to allow the depths of your awareness to come to the forefront of your consciousness, transforming your actions and leading to positive outcomes. It is possible to effect transformation in the world from the inside out, by realigning your highest thoughts and ideas with God's purpose. This involves accepting yourself as worthy of love, kindness, and respect in all that you seek on this earthly plane. With God's help, you can realize the changes you desire through cultivating your inner light and love of God.

Celebrations help us to count our blessings and give thanks to God.

WEEK TWO

THE ANGEL OF CELEBRATION

Joyful ceremonies or festivities help us to express our gratitude to God for the gift of our life, for the blessing of the people we love, and to mark those occasions that are special to us. We celebrate in order to raise our spirits, and to acknowledge the deeper meaning of life in everything we do. The act of celebration acknowledges God as central to our personal lives, and to the entire symphony of life. You may want to celebrate with gestures of generosity, acts of kindness, or special tokens of gratitude. Whatever the form, whether large or small—a balloon, a flower, a meal, a candle— your own celebration tells the world that today has, for you, a special meaning. When you celebrate life, you are affirming creation and confirming your worth as a child of God. In doing this, you open yourself to unlimited joy and love.

MEDITATION

See yourself as an angel looking down on humanity. You see unhappy people, suffering physical, spiritual, and emotional distress, and you want to help brighten their lives. Now use your creative skills to find a way to celebrate life that will affirm your own experience and touch the lives of those near to you. When you celebrate, you release the angel in you to make a difference in the lives of others. We can celebrate any day to make it special for ourselves and others. What are you going to do today to celebrate life?

Prayer

*O, Angel of Celebration,
open our hearts to the joy in our lives.
Let us celebrate the people and events
that mark our highest good
and greatest joy.
Teach us to celebrate our being,
our knowing, and our uniqueness.
Help us to mark our communion with God,
and to love life fully.
Amen.*

Joy is the loving and expansive expression of our unbound nature.

WEEK THREE

THE ANGEL OF JOY

Joy is our natural condition when we are free of the impediments that block vitality, awareness, and reverence for life. Far more than the mere absence of pain, confusion, or want, it is confirmation of our ability to love the absolute goodness and beauty of our lives. Joy is felt in the heart, and expressed through tears, laughter, touch, and a deep sense of gratitude. Remembering joyful times can lift our spirits when we are low. It teaches us to savor every moment when our hearts are free and our minds unburdened. Joy is a state of heightened affirmation and, perhaps, the closest we can get in this life to that pure state of bliss we call heaven.

MEDITATION

Find the place in your heart where moments of great joy live on. Bring these moments slowly to the surface of your consciousness and rekindle the experience in your mind's eye. Think of the times when you experienced such joy that you wept from the intensity, and remember feeling that joy was the holiest of emotions. When you do what makes your heart sing, you invite joy into your life. Open yourself to more of what you love, and you will be in that state of joy often.

Prayer

*Beloved Angel of Joy,
awaken our hearts to the joy of life.
Let us love and open ourselves to your presence
at all times.
Protect the joyful and preserve their innocence.
Remind us that our natural state is one of
harmony and grace.
Help us reaffirm the pure state of joy in all that
we are and all that we do.
Amen.*

LOVE AND PITY MEET THESE TWO
EVER WALK THE WORLD WITH YOU

Recreation is as vital for the health of our spirits as it is for our bodies.

WEEK FOUR

THE ANGEL OF RECREATION

Recreation suggests ease and pleasure at the release of tension and pressure. We all need time to unwind, smell the roses, and enjoy the fruits of a well-earned break from routine tasks. As we approach the summer solstice, our spirits lift, and our thoughts turn cheerfully to different kinds of relaxation and fun. The warmth and ease of long, light-filled days invite us to engage in pleasurable activity. Recreation helps us to refresh our bodies and spirits, and expands our sense of well-being. This is the season in which to take pleasure, whether we choose a physically or mentally challenging activity, or an easy, restful, or amusing pastime. We can delight in ourselves, in the beauty of nature, and in the life-giving power of the sun to store energy in our cells. It is time to recharge and regenerate on all levels of our being.

MEDITATION

See yourself doing the things that delight you. Whatever you fancy, let it be the basis for your desire for pleasure. Allow yourself to do what you enjoy and enhance your sense of well-being. It will help you to regenerate yourself at the deepest level. Look within; see yourself expanding with the pleasure and ease of summer. Let the good times charge your cells with positive energy and fill those reserves that you will need to call upon when life becomes stressful.

Gemini

Prayer

*Dearest Angel of
Recreation,
spark our sense of
fun, and remove any
ideas that limit our
delight.
Show us that a
measure of pleasure
and enjoyment make
a wholesome recipe
for health.
Thank you for the
sweetness of this time
of year for leisure and
regeneration.
Amen.*

Summer

In summer the spirit expands and rises toward the radiant light of God's love.

The summer solstice, about June 21, is ruled by the Archangel Uriel, who offers us the light of God.

The summer solstice, the point at which the sun is furthest from the equator, gives us the longest day and the shortest night of the year. On this joyful day, as our bodies receive the fullest measure of daylight, we become aware of the sun's capacity to warm and energize us, and of the powerful healing properties of light. The sun influences us on a spiritual as well as a physical level, for its energy makes us radiant, luminous, and resplendent. As we welcome summer into our hearts, we let its warmth and light lift us. Our spirits grow lighter, and soar toward the inner light of God's love.

The longest day was traditionally celebrated with bonfires, symbolizing the passion of our inner light, its illumination and knowledge. We have the opportunity at this high point of the year to awaken our heartfelt desire for love, happiness, and prosperity, and to fulfill our promise.

MEDITATION

This is a time to reconnect with your inner sun, which is always radiant and open to experiencing your highest good and greatest joy. Kindle the fire of your heart's desire, and see a pure light within yourself, which responds to your deepest longings. Let it burn away all impurities until you are left with the essence of your being, and the true experience of your Self. See the flame of this inner fire lighting your path through life, and ask yourself if you are fulfilling your higher purpose. If it is burning away the impediments between you and your higher purpose, you have brought the Archangel Uriel into your consciousness. When this burning is complete, you will know your true Self as a child of God.

JULEN 1927

ALLERS FAMILJ-JOURNAL

Prayer

*Dearest Uriel,
harbinger of God's
light and radiance,
we invite you to
kindle the spark of
passion to know, love,
and serve God.
Burn away the dross
of impurities that
darken our spirit.
Let doubt, fear,
arrogance, and lust
be banished, so that
our goodness shines.
Cast off the veil that
separates us from
our knowing,
so that our path is
illuminated.
Be our guide into the
land of light,
and our beacon when
life is dark.
Amen.*

The Archangel Uriel

Uriel leads the angelic armies, and stands before the Throne of Glory in heaven. His name means "Light of God," and he represents the light of God's teaching. Uriel is synonymous with our passion to unite with the Source. He is called the Flame of God, the Angel of the Presence, and Archangel of Salvation. In the Bible, he chastized Moses, and parted the Red Sea. He illuminated Ezra's prophetic visions. In the Book of Enoch he watches over thunder and terror, and elsewhere he is seen as the Angel of Repentance. He is thought to be the Prince of Lights referred to in one of the Dead Sea scrolls.

In the Catholic tradition, Uriel was the angel who guarded the gates of Eden with a fiery sword. Others believe that he guided Abraham out of Ur, and gave men the knowledge of Alchemy and the Kabbalah. Jews inscribed his name on amulets to help them in their study of the Torah. Uriel's energy is radiant, and is believed in some occult circles to be the antidote to radiation. In the Church, he is portrayed symbolically as an open hand holding a flame. He offers mankind the gift of enlightenment, which is the realization of Divinity within oneself.

	Cancer June 22–July 22	Leo July 23–August 22	Virgo August 23–September 22
ELEMENT	Water	Fire	Earth
COLOR	Yellow-orange	Yellow-gold	Lime Green
RULING PLANET	The Moon	The Sun	The Earth
PART OF BODY	The breast and the stomach	The back and the heart	The viscera
ANGEL	*The Angel of Discernment*	*The Angel of Worth*	*The Angel of Peace*
FESTIVALS	ST. JOHN'S FEAST *The Angel of Illumination*	THE ASSUMPTION OF THE VIRGIN *The Angel of Grace*	

ANGEL OF THE WEEK

WEEK 1	*The Angel of Knowledge*	*The Angel of Self-Approval*	*The Angel of Serenity*
WEEK 2	*The Angel of Intuition*	*The Angel of Self-Esteem*	*The Angel of Harmony*
WEEK 3	*The Angel of Imagination*	*The Angel of Self-Confidence*	*The Angel of Rest*
WEEK 4	*The Angel of Awareness*	*The Angel of Personal Power*	*The Angel of Pleasure*

Cancer

ELEMENT: *Water*

COLOR: *Yellow-orange*

RULING PLANET: *The Moon*

FESTIVAL: *St. John's Feast*

ANGEL: *The Angel of Discernment*

June 22–July 22

The long, golden days of summer increase our opportunities for ease and pleasure, giving us many more ways to enjoy the abundance of nature, and a greater variety of outdoor activities, seasonal foods, and forms of entertainment. This wealth of possibilities allows us the freedom to choose activities that serve our highest good, giving us both pleasure and peace, a choice that requires discernment.

Discernment is the ability to choose, in all circumstances, what is good for us. It is the judgment that unerringly distinguishes between what is really good and what, or who, simply looks or sounds good. This ability to discern the true path develops with life experience. It can save us from unnecessary difficulties, from unwholesome temptations and misguided entanglements, and keep us directed toward fulfilling our goals and dreams. Discernment means that we value who we are, and place our time, energy, and talents where they do the most good. It looks at all the options, considers them wisely, and flows with the one that brings optimal goodness, growth, and healing.

MEDITATION

Cultivating discernment requires that we be willing to look at our options. Staying aware, with an attuned mind, helps us to make wholesome choices. Think of a situation in which you are called upon to make a choice. You can move in one direction or another. Which of the two do you feel would have long-term benefits for your spiritual growth and wholeness? If you have trouble in making up your mind, pray to God for guidance and sound judgment. By using prayer, the highest operating principle, discernment will be yours.

Prayer

*Dearest Angel of
Discernment,
be a light on our path
to show us the way
of our highest good
and greatest joy.
Be a focal point of
choice and help us to
develop our capacity
to discern so that our
potential can be
realized.
Stimulate our higher
mind to choose the
right path for
our healing and
growth.
Amen.*

WEEK ONE

The gift of knowledge can be harnessed to our higher good.

THE ANGEL OF KNOWLEDGE

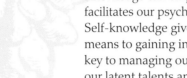

Prayer

O, Angel of Knowledge,
teach us to honor the light that
knowledge brings us.
Connect knowledge to our higher purpose,
and let it serve our evolution.
Teach us to combine the use of knowledge
with love, unity, and service
for a spiritual outcome for all humanity.
Spare us abuse of the power of knowledge,
and let us keep our self-knowing congruent
with our external knowledge.
Amen.

Knowledge can empower us. In the service of our higher mind, it facilitates our psychological growth and spiritual development. Self-knowledge gives us access to our own divinity, and is the means to gaining inner and outer freedom. Wisely used, it is the key to managing our lives, enabling us to recognize and develop our latent talents and skills.

Knowledge comes from God to enlighten humanity and support our spirit. It can help us to preempt or eliminate struggles, and to see where we are meant to be, and what we should be doing. When it serves our highest purpose we succeed in our endeavors. At its best, the power of knowledge enables us to realize our potential, and makes our minds capable of luminosity.

MEDITATION

It is said that knowledge accumulated over the ages can be accessed by the human mind, and that in each of us there is a part of the higher mind that has the ability to retrieve this information. Is there a particular form of knowledge that would serve you now in your development? You can find answers to many questions through meditation and prayer. Sit quietly, and ask your higher mind to give you the answers to the problems and issues affecting your life. Trust in your mind's ability to tap into this vast well of knowledge and serve your greatest good.

*Intuition is a way
of knowing that
connects you to
the truth.*

WEEK TWO

THE ANGEL
OF INTUITION

Intuition is instinctive knowledge or insight that comes not by rational intelligence but by direct experience, and reflects our ability to know what we can know deeply and truly. It is how the angels speak to us, and how we know God's desire for our joy and happiness. It is through intuition that we access our inner truth and align our personality with our Divine nature.

In order to fulfill your creative destiny, it is important that you trust your intuition. Listening to your intuition will help you to find guidance. Angels often communicate with humans through symbols, metaphors, and visions, which need to be interpreted. Intuition is the means by which they are understood, the faculty linking you with the realm of spirit. Intuition comes out of your deepest connection with God, and can help you to make wholesome decisions for your life.

Prayer

*Blessed Angel of Intuition,
open our intuition to know that
which we can know.
Speak to us so that we can acknowledge
your presence.
Show us visions of possibilities that will open
up new horizons in our lives.
Deepen our trust in our inner light,
and help us to make healthy choices
for ourselves.
Let us know the importance of
trusting our intuition to guide us
on our path in life.
Amen.*

MEDITATION

Focus your mind and ask yourself what you know about your health. What do you need to do to improve it? What do you know about your friendships and relationships? What needs changing in these areas? What do you know about your finances? What needs attending to here? Intuition is a tool that can make a big difference in your life. Choose to develop it by recognizing what you do know. You may surprise yourself.

TO THE GLORY OF GOD AND IN MEMORY OF ANNE
KINDNESS AND MEEKNESS AND COMFORT

Imagination enables us to envisage the future we want.

THE ANGEL OF IMAGINATION

Prayer

*Beloved Angel of Imagination,
rekindle the spirit of imagination in our lives.
Help us to reanimate our visions and dreams,
in order to see the future we wish to have.
Awaken our spirit to the fulfillment of our
greatest possibilities.
Help us to see ourselves as happy,
loved, and whole.
Amen.*

Imagination is a gift from our minds. It gives us the ability to form an internal picture of the components needed for our greater good. Cultivating imagination is a wonderful way to enhance the things that delight and enchant us. It helps us to actualize our heart's desires. It is often suppressed when we are young because it gets in the way of "earthly learning," or the acquisition of skills that teachers and parents think are important to help us achieve in life. But without imagination, we are unable to see the future we wish to create for ourselves. The faculty of imagination is heightened in great thinkers, visionaries, and creative people. It can be activated by right-brain functions such as music, dance, painting, and daydreaming. When it is linked with our deepest desires, it gives us the ability to manifest our intentions in reality.

MEDITATION

Use the power of your imagination to change your experience of life. In your mind's eye, see yourself as healthy and happy, and doing the things you love. Imagine yourself being fulfilled in every way. Imagine being at peace, in a place you enjoy, surrounded by people who love you.

Take time every day to imagine these things. You may find that they come to pass easily, and are quickly a part of your life experience.

Angels of the week

Prayer

Beloved Angel of Awareness,
open our eyes to the glory of God,
and show us the realms of possibility
that await us.
You are the gift that takes us into
the world of choices.
Help us see what is, and to embrace life with
greater love and compassion.
Bless us that we may awaken to a higher
consciousness.
Amen.

Heightened awareness opens the door to realms of possibility.

WEEK FOUR

THE ANGEL OF AWARENESS

Awareness is the knowledge of ourselves and the world around us. It is the state of being awakened, in which the mind sees, experiences, and grasps a new level of reality. Higher levels of awareness develop at each stage of our lives, so that with time we gain a deep and essential understanding of our true natures, as well as of our unfolding purpose.

Awareness is the key to how life can best be cherished and brought to fruition, with soul and spirit in harmony. Heightened awareness is the door through which our mind can pass into the realms of possibility, where all things can be achieved and we can choose how we wish to live and experience life. The awakening of our consciousness of the greater reality sets us free.

MEDITATION

Bring yourself into a state of awareness and scan your body. Explore it to see where your energy is flowing, and where it is blocked and congested. As you focus on yourself with this exercise, your awareness becomes heightened, and it becomes a state of "knowing." You can direct this consciousness to your body, to your emotions, or to your thoughts and spirituality. Your awareness is a gift from God, enabling you to know yourself, and to explore the world around you.

Leo

July 23–August 22

ELEMENT: *Fire*

COLOR: *Yellow-gold*

RULING PLANET: *The Sun*

FESTIVAL: *The Assumption of the Virgin*

ANGEL: *The Angel of Worth*

Prayer

Beloved Angel of Worth,
banish doubts about our
worthiness.
Show us God's unconditional love.
Teach us to align ourselves with
His will, so that we can realize our
desires and help to heal the world.
Let us know our true worth as
reflections of God's light.
Amen.

At the height of summer the strength of the sun illuminates the earth and nourishes our spirits. Our inner sense of Self blossoms and our own light shines forth. We know that we are worthy of what we say we want. We love and accept ourselves unconditionally in the full light of these warm summer days. Nothing can separate us from the knowledge of God's love. We are worthy because we exist, and there is nothing we need to do, think, feel, or be, in order to receive His love.

Known as king of the zodiac, the fiery sign of Leo delights in an expanded spirit. Its characteristics are power, assertiveness, extroversion, expressiveness, and spontaneity. We can affirm the power of Leo within us by allowing our internal sun to shine more brightly. We can become noble and eloquent in our resolve to fulfill the best in ourselves, becoming a beacon for others, and so expressing our worth and honoring our choices for love.

MEDITATION

The center of self-worth and personal confidence is in the solar plexus, in the pit of the stomach, an area that grows tight and constricted whenever we feel fearful or worried. As you breathe in, release any tension you may feel here. Visualize a sphere of yellow-golden light and place it in this center. Let this light fill and warm your body. Expand and intensify it as you release deeply held tension. This will bring healing to weakened confidence or a diminished sense of self. Let the light radiate into your abdomen and thorax. See it as a radiant sun shining wherever you direct your attention, warming, soothing, healing the wounds of self-doubt and anxiety. You will come to know your true value as a person cherished and loved by God.

*Self-approval is
an expression of
our sharing in
God's love.*

Prayer

*Dear Angel of Self-approval,
heal the wounds of our separation from
our true Self.
Expand our approval in the light of who
we truly are.
Help us to reconstruct the temple of our inner
light through loving and accepting ourselves
as our heavenly father loves
and approves of us.
Amen.*

WEEK ONE

THE ANGEL OF SELF-APPROVAL

Self-approval means that we accept both our limitations and our talents and gifts with love and kindness. If we do not like who we are, or approve of our actions, how can we expect anyone else to approve of us? The responsibility for transforming how we think of ourselves is up to us. If we are dependent upon others to define us, we are giving away our power. Only we can define our innate worth and value as individuals. When we approve of who we are, we re-parent ourselves, consciously healing any damage to our self-esteem, and building a resilient and realistic ego that can cope with life's challenges. It may take a lifetime of self-affirmation to open up the channels of love, goodness, and healing that we deserve. Let us learn to define ourselves in the light of God's love for us, which is eternal, constant, and unconditional.

MEDITATION

Self-approval means treating yourself with kindness, and building on your strengths. Make approving of yourself a new habit in your daily routine. Look at the path of your life, the hardships, the trials, the fears, the limitations, and approve of who you are and what you have done to give your life meaning and quality. Stop yourself each time you find a reason to hate yourself. Self-approval becomes an exercise in unconditional love. Transform your mind with love and approve of who you are. You are, after all, worth it.

Self-esteem is the affirmation of our acceptance of our worth.

Prayer

*Beloved Angel of Self-esteem,
seal the door where negativity dwells.
Direct us to the place within, where we are
naturally proud.
Let our self-esteem act as a wholesome
boundary to protect and honor the child
of God within us.
Our worth is His, and our esteem
sings His praise.
Amen.*

WEEK TWO

THE ANGEL OF SELF-ESTEEM

Self-esteem is generated by our sense of worth, knowing that who we are and what we do has validity. The wholesome pride we take in what we have done with our lives is the result of choosing to accept ourselves in a positive and affirming way. We can all find reason to think well of ourselves when looking at our record in human terms and acknowledging the unforced acts of kindness, open-heartedness, and gentleness that we have shown.

This recognition of our own virtues is a tribute to our shared divinity. We develop self-esteem when we honor ourselves by being true to our inner light, and do what we know needs to be done, regardless of the circumstances. Every time that we affirm ourselves we grow in self-esteem.

MEDITATION

Know that you are a creature of light, and that you reflect the inner light of God within you. It is strong, resilient, and can penetrate any darkness, no matter how dense. This is the light that fires your self-esteem, which shines whenever you know how good you truly are. Reflect on your life and remember the occasions when you went beyond your limitations. Say "yes" to the times you found that you liked yourself, and were proud of what you did to make your corner of the universe a better place.

Prayer

*O, Angel of Self-
confidence,
teach us to balance
our gifts and abilities
with God's grace.
Show us what we are
capable of, and how
to accept our talents
with humility.
Build our confidence
so that we can trust
in our good.
Help us to fulfill our
purpose, and others
to find their abilities.
Teach us that it is
acceptable to know
that we are truly
good.
Amen.*

Self-confidence comes from knowing that our lives are blessed.

WEEK THREE

THE ANGEL OF SELF-CONFIDENCE

Self-confidence is based on the realization that we are able to live happy and productive lives, that we are capable of being and doing the right thing, and of accomplishing what we set out to do with energy, verve, and enthusiasm. It comes from knowing that who we are and what we do is enough, and is grounded in a positive and realistic appreciation of our self-worth and abilities. Knowing that our lives are blessed and protected allows us to live in ease and ensures that our efforts will be fruitful. Confidence gives us an inner peace that lets our energy flow freely in the direction we are taking. It is not congested with fear or doubt.

Confidence in ourselves reflects the greater operating principle known as Divine Intelligence or the Christ Light. If we become egocentric, we lose touch with its Source. When we combine our ability with God's help, our lives unfold gracefully.

MEDITATION

As you turn your thoughts inward, allow yourself to be confident in your natural ability to be and to do the best that you can. Believe in yourself and in your life's path. You know that you are truly good and doing the best you can. Let your confidence expand. God and the angels are on your side, helping you to fulfill your purpose in life.

Prayer

*Dearest Angel of
Personal Power,
you are always
helping us strive to be
the best that
we can.
You remind us that
God has need of us on
a higher plane,
and you guide us,
when life feels fearful,
to take the next step
forward.
Direct us to those
who challenge us to
be empowered,
and to stand for the
light, the truth,
and the good.
Help us to develop
power in safe and
wholesome ways,
never abusing it,
but recognizing God
within every soul.
Empower us with
strength, grace,
and love.
Amen.*

Personal power can transform the world through the realization of Self.

WEEK FOUR

THE ANGEL OF PERSONAL POWER

Personal power reflects your ability to be yourself in any context. It comes from knowing and trusting in yourself, and is a synthesis of all that you are, strong and weak, good and less than perfect. It is a quality that carries the gravity of your experience, your accumulated wisdom, and your personal presence. It shines when you are clear about your worth and your abilities. This attribute is perceived by the world as integrity, clarity, honesty, and sincerity. It is a composite of all that is positive, good, clear, and focused. Its energy will have been generated and formed by the trials and tests of your life.

Personal power differs from other forms of power in that it does not depend on other people for its expression. It is the ability to transform yourself and the world around you simply by being yourself. To sustain it requires vigilance, discipline, and constancy in maintaining your vision and living your truth.

MEDITATION

Reflect on the nature of personal power. Project your awareness of this into your thoughts and tell yourself that you can build personal power with God's help. The clarity of your intention to live from your highest truth empowers you to grow in quantum leaps, and catapults you to a higher level of personal responsibility. This requires you to own your power, and to acknowledge the Holy Spirit as your sustaining force.

Virgo

ELEMENT: *Earth*

COLOR: *Lime Green*

RULING PLANET: *The Earth*

ANGEL: *The Angel of Peace*

With the fullness of the year we feel nourished and rested. We have stored light in our cells for the winter months, and our spirits are refreshed. On these days of high summer we can relax and find peace of mind, a state that reflects our acceptance of ourselves and of what life brings. When we are open to self-knowledge, to loving life, and to being at one with God's will, our souls know the "peace ... which passeth all understanding."

Virgo is associated with the earth and fertility. At this time of year, plants and crops are ripe and at their prime, just before the autumn harvest. It is a season of maturity and plenty, in which to enjoy the fruits of one's labor. Virgo encourages activities that require creativity, precision, and perfection. This is manifested at a material level through attention to detail, and at a spiritual level through the acceptance of growth and change. Inner peace is the fruit of practice, and of the decision to process all experience.

MEDITATION

There is within each of us a place where there is neither conflict nor attachment, where peace, freedom, and love exist. This is the level of being where you are truly yourself, deeply at one with your essential spirit. Do not search for this place within yourself; it already exists. Rather allow yourself to be that which you seek. Choose to be peace, and experience your whole being responding in a positive and wholesome way as you become that which you desire. Choose peace, and be at one with yourself. Choose peace, and watch as your tension melts under the intensity of your own natural warmth and sweetness. This is the inner harvest of your labor and practice of looking within.

*O, Angel of Peace,
we call upon you in
the midst of turmoil
and confusion to
bring harmony to
our thoughts.
Peace is a gift from
God, that blesses the
gates of our homes,
our work, our schools
and institutions.
Let peace be the focus
of our activities, and
may we live gently
under its shelter.
Amen.*

*Conflict dissolves
and serenity comes
when we are at one
with our true Self.*

WEEK ONE

THE ANGEL
OF SERENITY

Prayer

*Beloved Angel of Serenity,
touch our lives more frequently.
As your blessing sweetens our life,
remind us always to welcome you.
You soothe our tired minds and awaken our
longing for peace.
Help us to surrender to God's will so that we
may delight in His peace.
Amen.*

Serenity flows from the attunement of our minds and bodies with our higher self. More than tranquility, it resonates from the deep center of our spirit to bring peace, contentment, purpose, and fulfillment. Serenity is an aspect of the Crown Chakra, the highest power center of the body in yoga, where we confirm our indelible connection with the Source.

We invite serenity into our lives when we choose to live by the highest spiritual principles, letting go of conflict and allowing the Holy Spirit to take command of our destiny. The calm and clarity of serenity come to us when our will is united with the will of the Divine, and we know that we are in the right place, doing the right thing. As we let go of stress and tension we are filled with a delicious feeling of ease. This is a blissful state, in which we are at one with all life. Serenity is ours when we place our trust in God, in the light of whose love we can do our best in every situation.

MEDITATION

Visualize the color violet and feel it cloak you with bright, calm, protective energy. Now allow yourself to feel serenity by letting go and relaxing. Stay in this state for as long as you feel the need. You can draw on it whenever you feel stressed or plagued with problems. By developing this skill of visualizing the color violet, you will be able to recall the feelings associated with it and to enjoy moments of complete serenity at any time.

Harmony is equilibrium, the healing balance of being and doing.

WEEK TWO

THE ANGEL OF HARMONY

Prayer

Beloved Angel of Harmony, we know that for you to be a part of our lives we need to clear a space for you. When we clutter our days with activities that cost time and energy, we lose you. Show us the balance between being and doing, and bring harmony and healing into our lives. Amen.

Harmony is that balanced state where our emotions are still, our minds clear, and our bodies in tune with our intentions. It takes effort to achieve this apparent ease, and to bring balance into the world around us. Harmony is a reflection of our intention to be at peace and at one with ourselves, others, and the environment. It comes to us when we stop pushing and striving, and fall back into a pace that resonates with our natural rhythms and cycles. It is generated by the balancing of our external activities with our inner world of self-conscious awareness. When we are set on "doingness," we miss out on that quality of "beingness" that comes when we are still, and in tune with our true nature.

Finding the balance between doing and being can be difficult in the hectic modern world that demands so much tension, stamina, and energy from us. Taking time to be with ourselves, to be in nature, or to be silent in our tasks, can refresh our spirits with a deep sense of harmony.

MEDITATION

Envisage yourself being in harmony with your immediate environment and with nature. When you feel this you will be more at one with yourself. Consider which areas of your life are in need of harmony. How do you envision inner and outer harmony reigning in your circumstances? If you truly desire it, harmony will find its way into your life.

Rest helps both mind and body to stay in harmony with nature.

WEEK THREE

THE ANGEL OF REST

Few people pay more than lip service to the idea of rest, even though it is known to be vital to health and well-being. We all occasionally need to pause in our exertions, to unplug from the intensity of our daily lives, and to let our bodies and minds recharge. Without relaxation, the body breaks down and our thinking becomes muddled. We lose clarity and focus, and end up feeling physically and mentally exhausted. Rest enables our systems to function optimally, and gives us an opportunity to reflect on new possibilities.

If you honor your need to rest, you will stay in harmony with yourself and nature. Rest will renew your spirit and replenish your reserves of vitality to be drawn upon when you need them.

Prayer

*Beloved Angel of Rest,
you bring the joy of peace to ease our tired bodies and refresh our weary minds.
Teach us to listen to our bodies and to know when to stop.
Revive our spirits when the world pulls us into its vortex.
Teach us to respect the importance of rest in our lives.
Amen.*

MEDITATION

Listen to your body and feel the need to unwind. Lie on your back with your knees up, and with your head resting on a thick book, placed under the ridge at the base of the skull. Imagine gravity pulling the muscles of your back down. This will relax it. Lie there for approximately 20 minutes and visualize your back lengthening and widening. This exercise rests your spine and helps to release deep muscular tension. Doing it regularly, once a day, enables your body to benefit from scheduled rest. Stop pushing yourself when you are tired, and help yourself to regenerate.

Pleasure heightens our perceptions and frees the spirit.

WEEK FOUR

THE ANGEL OF PLEASURE

Pleasure is what we feel when the heart, mind, and senses combine to experience joy and delight. It is always simple, and contains the possibility of expansion and gratitude. The sensation of physical pleasure makes the cells in our body expand; pain causes them to contract. On a spiritual level, pleasure releases the soul to soar to new heights of beauty and awareness. This ability to delight in creation is God-given, and can sustain us in adversity.

Because our five senses respond joyfully to agreeable stimuli, it is likely that we are meant to enjoy the profuse delights of sound, vision, touch, taste, and scent. As our bodies are designed to experience pleasure, it surely follows that our will is intended not to suppress, but to fulfill our desires. Perhaps it is time to reevaluate pleasure, to trust in the judgment of our hearts and in our ability to find the right balance between restraint and pleasure.

Prayer

Dearest Angel of Pleasure,
enable us to stop punishing ourselves.
Show us the fair measure of
what is truly good for us.
Make us aware of pleasure in ways
that are respectful.
Teach us that pleasure is good
for the spirit,
so that we may learn how to
enjoy ourselves.
Amen.

MEDITATION

Pleasure is often found in small things that stimulate the senses. Ask yourself to what degree you are willing to allow more pleasure into your life. Can you turn ordinary tasks into pleasure? Can you regard your daily routines as pleasurable? Pleasure is as much an attitude as an experience. When you choose to see the infinite possibilities for pleasure, you open yourself to more of what you really want, and learn to delight in the ordinary things of life.

Autumn

As the year turns, we count our blessings and dedicate ourselves to the light of truth.

The autumn equinox, about September 22, is ruled by the Archangel Michael, who brings us the love of God.

The autumn equinox is the halfway point between summer and winter, when the retreating sun crosses the celestial equator, and day and night are again of equal length. This is a moment of balance and harmony, when our personal identity is partially connected with the outer world and partially focused inward. Just as light and darkness are evenly balanced, so our psyche embraces the two approaches of linear rationality and cyclical emotion in equal measure. The heavens display the sign of the Scales to notify us that all is in order in the universe.

Autumn is the time of harvest, when the seeds we have planted mature and ripen, and we reap what we have sown. Leaves change color, the days begin to shorten, and our spirits naturally turn inward toward the Self. We appraise our strengths and weaknesses, and strive to develop the virtues of a gracious spirit and personal integrity.

Autumn is also a time for knowing where we stand and what we stand for. The seasonal festivals are a testament to the quickening of our spiritual awareness. Michaelmas, Rosh Hashanah, and Yom Kippur are ancient holy days that renew our covenant with the living God within us to live consciously and to fulfill our deepest potential for good.

MEDITATION

Reflect on the changes you experience as the days become balanced. This is a good time to process any thoughts that disturb your equilibrium. The changing seasons also remind us of what is constant in our nature. Use this time to reflect on the eternal nature of spirit. Michael resonates with our higher mind, guiding us toward integrity, truth, and purity of spirit. Accept his guidance, and you will live in harmony with God's will.

Prayer

*O, Michael, Angel
of Fall,
help us to winnow
out negativity
and all dysfunctional
attitudes that dim
our radiant light.
Enable us to
surmount the
external changes that
confront us in
our lives,
and bring us to a
place of peace
where we are deeply
content with
ourselves.
Amen.*

The Archangel Michael

Michael is the most powerful of the angels, revered equally in the Jewish, Christian, and Moslem traditions. His name means "Who is as God?" His position in heaven is on the right of the Throne of Glory, and on earth at the right hand of man. He is chief of the archangels, head of the angelic order of Virtues, and ruler of the fourth heaven. Michael is the conqueror of Satan, and the defender of our integrity. He is God's great messenger of love and mercy, who leads the souls of the just to heaven.

In the Bible, Michael announced to Sarah that she would give birth to Isaac, prevented the sacrifice of Jacob, later wrestled with Jacob, and led the Israelites during their wandering in the wilderness. He is the Prince of Light in the Dead Sea scroll known as *The Wars of the Sons of Light against the Sons of Darkness*. Later, he was seen as the forerunner of the Shekhinah, and as the angel of the burning bush. There is a Christian tradition that Michael told the Virgin Mary of her approaching assumption; and a Moslem tradition that his tears, shed over the sins of the faithful, coalesced to form the cherubim.

Michael's powers of judgment are tempered by mercy. He champions the weak, and all who fight evil. At this time of year, when day and night are in perfect balance, he asks us to bring harmony and order into our lives, to avoid chaos as an invitation to evil, and to live in accordance with our highest principles. As the old year gives way to the new, Michael enables us to release outworn ideas and stale resentments, so that we can move on into the months ahead unburdened by anything that will weigh our spirit down.

	Libra September 23–October 22	Scorpio October 23–November 21	Sagittarius November 22–December 20
ELEMENT	Air	Water	Fire
COLOR	Forest Green	Aqua Blue	Blue
RULING PLANET	Venus	Pluto	Jupiter
PART OF BODY	The veins and the bladder	The reproductive organs	The hips and the thighs
ANGEL	*The Angel of Guidance*	*The Angel of Creativity*	*The Angel of Exploration*
FESTIVALS	MICHAELMAS *The Angel of Justice*	SUKKOT *The Angel of Permanence*	ADVENT *The Angel of Expectation*
	ROSH HASHANAH *The Angel Israel*	ALL SAINTS' DAY *The Angel of Good Deeds*	
	YOM KIPPUR *The Shekhinah*	ALL SOULS' DAY *The Angel of Divine Spirit*	
ANGEL OF THE WEEK			
WEEK 1	*The Angel of Truth*	*The Angel of Sensitivity*	*The Angel of Adventure*
WEEK 2	*The Angel of Courage*	*The Angel of Talents and Gifts*	*The Angel of Curiosity*
WEEK 3	*The Angel of Fortitude*	*The Angel of Apprenticeship*	*The Angel of Opportunity*
WEEK 4	*The Angel of Integrity*	*The Angel of Mastery*	*The Angel of Expansion*

Libra

ELEMENT: *Air*

COLOR: *Forest Green*

RULING PLANET: *Venus*

FESTIVALS: *Michaelmas*
Rosh Hashanah
Yom Kippur

ANGEL: *The Angel*
of Guidance

Libra is a time of balance, beauty, and harmony. Our psyche is balanced in its capacity to experience emotions and to evaluate situations. Each function of the mind, from rational computing and problem analysis to intuition and imagination, has equal sway within our personality. The days are evenly balanced, the seasons undergo their cyclical change, and we find our spirit free to delight in the grace, beauty, and serenity of an Indian summer, while managing to be disciplined, punctual, and orderly. Libra is also the sign of diplomacy, seeking balance in all situations where there is disharmony and conflict. It enjoys elegance and eloquence in all matters, especially those of the heart.

The Scales of Libra represent equality. The Libran in us loves esthetics, but can also stand up and fight for justice. At this time of year we discover our latent strength and intellectual power. The Angel of Guidance calls us to the path of our higher good, and lights the way ahead to give us the greatest possibility for growth, healing, and love. When we attune ourselves with its guidance, we are rewarded with experiences that show us the glory of God and teach us who we truly are at our source.

Prayer

Beloved Angel of Guidance,
we ask your favor in
leading us to the light of the Self.
Be a beacon to illuminate our way when we
are faced with the dark night of the soul.
Be there for us when we seek your help
during these fearful times.
Keep us from harm,
and show us how to follow
our heartfelt dreams to positive fruition.
Support us when we falter,
and help us to be good, loving, and true.
Amen.

MEDITATION

Reflect on the times that you were given guidance. How often can you recall having received a message to do something that turned out to be for your healing, good, or joy? Sit quietly and listen to your inner guide. It can lead you in the right direction and along the appropriate path. Trusting your internal guidance can save you time, money, and emotional pain. It comes in the form of dreams, meditations, and your inner knowing about any situation. Strengthening your inner guide, learning to listen to and to trust your intuition, takes patience and faith.

Truth frees our minds and hearts to see clearly and love greatly.

WEEK ONE

THE ANGEL OF TRUTH

Prayer

Blessed Angel of Truth,
bring the light of truth into our lives.
Help us in every situation to be honest.
Guide our hearts and minds to know that truth
is our salvation.
May our personal truth be honored by those
who love us.
Release any fear of truth so that we can live
openly and know healing.
Help us to discern truth from illusion,
and to value the ultimate truth of God, which
endures through all change.
Amen.

The truth is what is so for us in the here and now. The true perception of the present moment, however, reflects our deepest knowledge of both our local, personal self, and our Divine nature. When we are aware of the greater reality of who we are, the smaller, petty realities of life gain a different perspective.

When we accept the truth of our innermost feelings, our desires, fears, and doubts, we start to live more fully. Being truthful with ourselves opens up our energy fields, releasing an invigorating flow of vitality, and allowing healing to happen. When we are honest about our situations and circumstances, we are better able to find appropriate, positive, and wholesome answers to our needs. "The truth will set you free" describes the power of truth to liberate us from our delusions and to provide our lives with clarity and meaning. This week let truth guide you in making healthy choices and wise decisions.

MEDITATION

Reflect on what the truth means to you. Truth is deep and can cause you to question what you really value in life. It is important to ask yourself how truthful you are, to yourself and to others, about the things and people you care about. Hold the concept of truth in your mind and connect it to your heart. It will set you free from the illusions that limit your joy and your sense of worth, and open your heart to healing.

Angels of the week

We can take heart in God's help when holding to the truth.

WEEK TWO

THE ANGEL OF COURAGE

The Angel of Courage is Adriel, whose name means "my help is God." One of the angelic guards of the gates of the South Wind, he testifies to our highest ideals. It takes courage to live for ourselves, and to do what we know to be right.

Living with integrity, with the courage of our convictions, can put us in conflict with others who may feel that they know better than we do what is good for us. Courage is often called for to complete an unpleasant or difficult task, or to combat a debilitating illness. The Angel of Courage teaches us to trust that whatever happens we will be cared for. Armed with this knowledge, we can face life through its uncertainties, and hold fast to our trust in Divine providence. Courage is granted to all who put their faith in God and seek His help.

Prayer

O, Angel of Courage,
Empower us to face those who instill
fear, doubt, and worry.
Guide us toward our highest good,
and give us the courage to complete our life's
journey with our spirit intact.
Let us know courage so that we can summon it
from the depths of our soul
whenever we need it.
Amen.

MEDITATION

Reflect on your feelings about courage. Ask yourself whether you feel brave enough to live your life the way you want. Courage will come to you when you invoke God's help. Remember that you do not have to be fearless or undaunted by life's trials, only willing and able to move through challenging times doing the best you can. It takes courage to follow your heart in life. With faith in your connection with the Divine mind, reach deep inside yourself and harness the courage to do the things you enjoy, and be the person you would truly like to be.

Fortitude comes from facing crisis and conflict resolutely.

WEEK THREE

THE ANGEL OF FORTITUDE

We are not born with fortitude but learn it as we are forced to deal with life's challenges. Through life we develop fortitude. It teaches us about the better part of ourselves. It strengthens us and enables us to endure and ground ourselves in our highest truth. Fortitude helps us complete the tasks that are important to us. It is a quality known to the wise and mature and combines a mixture of patience and presence, of knowing when to relax and rest and when to forge ahead. Nothing of any real significance gets done without it.

MEDITATION

Think about a time in your life when you knew you needed to see something through to a proper conclusion. Did you do whatever it took to finish this task? If so, you must have been proud of yourself. This is how we develop maturity and fortitude.

As you look within, know that you have what it takes to complete any task you set your mind to do. It may require long hours, great expense, and even sacrifice, but you know that, if necessary, and with God's help, you can do what it takes.

Prayer

We pray to the Angel of Fortitude. Help us transform tendencies to give up, and assist us in completing our tasks. Give us the fortitude to see our dreams become reality, and enable us to see positive outcomes. Amen.

WEEK FOUR

THE ANGEL OF INTEGRITY

Prayer

We pray to the Angel of Integrity.
Help us keep our covenant with God to be honest, loyal, and whole.
We ask to evolve consciously by living from our integrity.
Guide us to make wholesome choices that serve our growth and honor our core.
Strengthen our integrity when it would be easy to follow the crowd rather than stand for what we know to be right.
Help us to honor this basic truth of Self.
Amen.

Integrity refers to our ability to honor our words and actions, so that we are congruent in what we say and do. Having integrity means we respect our spirit in every action we take. We treat all people as brothers or sisters, and we honor their spirits in the way we would like our spirit honored.

People who have integrity can be counted on to do their best in every situation. Integrity makes the difference between being ordinary and being excellent. It is the natural consequence of being truly anchored in our own Divine nature.

MEDITATION

Reflect on your ability to "walk your talk." This refers to an impeccable spirit aligned to a profound sense of truth. This means that we do what we say we will do. What we say carries weight and substance. As you look within your self, see if you say things you mean and keep the promises you make to the best of your ability.

Whenever we lie, or fail to honor our inner truth, we separate ourselves from this place of radiance within. We fall into the shadowy places that lie within all of us, and allow this darkness to dominate. Let your light shine by striving to be whole, complete, and a source of integrity. Believe in yourself as trustworthy, honorable, and true.

Scorpio

October 23–November 21

ELEMENT: *Water*

COLOR: *Aqua Blue*

RULING PLANET: *Pluto*

FESTIVALS: *Sukkot*

All Saints' Day

All Souls' Day

ANGEL: *The Angel of Creativity*

Our natural capacity for creativity is our most endearing gift from God. It enables us to express the best of ourselves in endless forms and through a variety of experiences. When we are creative, life energy courses through us; it is indelibly linked to our soul's path. Our spirit shines and longs to fulfill itself through the medium that we feel best expresses us.

We are meant to be creative in all aspects of our lives. The creative drive helps to attune us to whatever may be in need of uplifting, clarifying, polishing, or healing within us. Staying creative transforms the old into the new; it regenerates our spirit in a continuous cycle that defies age, class, or wealth.

We are creative in order to fulfill ourselves. Once you open your channels to Divine energy by allowing your creativity to flourish, your life will never be the same. You will experience ultimate fulfillment, joy, and delight. Find out what makes your heart sing, and develop your talents and gifts until you are skilled in self-expression. Honor these precious gifts by seeing where best you can use them. Treat creativity as a valuable jewel: it is the life force manifesting through you. The Angel of Creativity asks to show you the very best of yourself in whatever field you choose.

MEDITATION

Allow yourself to imagine how much joy is available to you when you open up your creative channels. You have the possibility to use your greatest gifts to enhance, inspire, and stimulate that part of you that is innovative and loves a creative act. Do you dare to become the creative person whom you know yourself to be? Creativity applies to every field of life; it is not limited to the arts. Use your creative gifts and value them. They come directly from the Source.

VICTOR CARPATHIVS
· M · D · X ·

Prayer

*Beloved Angel of
Creativity,
you are the energy
that gives life its
forms.
You show us the
colors and sing us
the tunes.
You show us the
dance and open up
the way for us to
express our very
nature.
Thank you for the
opportunities to
express so much joy
and imagination.
Creativity fulfills that
aspect of the Creator
within us all.
It is the greatest gift
we have,
next to life itself.
Amen.*

Your sensitivity to life's nuances is a gift that can enrich others.

WEEK ONE

THE ANGEL OF SENSITIVITY

Sensitivity arises from the depths of our nature. It suggests an awareness of and responsiveness to the world that is both refined and astute. Many people refuse to acknowledge how sensitive they are, for this quality can be both a blessing and a curse. If you are very conscious of your environment and of the changes occurring at subtle levels, but have no way of dealing with your feelings, then your sensitivity will feel like a burden. If you are comfortable expressing yourself, on the other hand, and have the support of a network of people who understand and appreciate your gifts, you will value your finely tuned awareness.

Give your feelings the space in which to develop and grow. You may develop particular skills that use your sensitivity wisely and are widely appreciated. Putting your sensitivity into the service of healing other people could be a way of channeling your gift into the world. Open your heart to the needs of others and cultivate your own responsiveness, and you will be granted guidance on how best to use your special talents.

Prayer

Dear Angel of Sensitivity, transform our pain into pleasure, and heal our hearts. Open our minds to healing. Let us develop a sensitivity so fine that we feel the suffering of others, as well as the world's beauty. Heighten our awareness of the joy of spirit, and enable us to use our gifts for healing and delight. Teach us to balance sensitivity with a resilient and wholesome ego, so as to sense the rightness of things. Amen.

MEDITATION

It is essential to expand your sensitivity to the highest plane, and not fix it on a lower level of suffering and pain. Channel your sensitivity into love and healing. Choose to place the gifts of your perceptiveness and awareness in the service of healing others. This will help to depersonalize your sensitivity, and provide you with greater balance and stability.

Angels of the week

Prayer

Dearest Angel of Talents and Gifts,
you see the blessing of our riches
long before we recognize them,
and you know they may lie dormant
until we are compelled
to express them.
Please help us to be aware of our gifts and
gently coax us
to develop those that will give us
the greatest joy and satisfaction
and bring healing
to others.
Many of us are blessed with a clear
message that we have something
very special to offer.
Lead us to the right people,
who will cherish us for who we are
and not exploit our gifts.
Help us to develop that part of ourselves
that is God-given, and show us how
to protect and nourish our gifts.
Amen.

God has blessed us with many talents and gifts, which often emerge as a great surprise.

WEEK TWO

THE ANGEL OF TALENTS AND GIFTS

We may not be aware that we have a special talent until a particular situation brings it to the surface. Sometimes we may recognize early on that a child has a great gift. We may push, cajole, and force him or her to express it, and in the process destroy the ability by suppressing the natural joy that accompanies it.

There is a Chinese expression that great gifts ripen late. When we mature into responsible adults, we develop the necessary discipline and rigor to bring latent talent to light and to nurture it.

Gifts for healing, therapy, art, writing, music, or oratory, to name but a few, take time and commitment to bear fruit. Honoring our gifts means taking ourselves seriously and learning to cherish what God has given us. Abusing a gift is the same as abusing God. It is important to surround yourself with people who see your gifts and encourage you to develop them.

MEDITATION

Reflect on your talents and gifts. Which of these do you value the most? Do you feel that there are new gifts emerging? Do you want to do something about this? Or simply let them emerge naturally? A common fear about a gift is that you may feel unable to support yourself. Begin to value your talents and gifts. They are God-given and have been passed down to you so that you can fulfill the intention they were designed to express. When you honor them you are celebrating the best part of yourself. You are saying that you take yourself seriously and want to live out this piece of divinity in you. It is never too late to honor what has been yours since birth. Affirm your talents and honor your gifts. They are meant to take you through life.

We are all given a period of grace in which to learn from our mistakes.

WEEK THREE

THE ANGEL OF APPRENTICESHIP

Once we decide to develop our talents and gifts, we need to undergo training in order to acquire and perfect our skills. The period in which we test what we have learned is traditionally known as apprenticeship. It gives us the opportunity to learn from our mistakes, and time to integrate our skills with the demands of new situations. We are not expected to be perfect, only to do our best. Few of us, however, are willing to accept this period of grace. Apprenticeship can be frustrating, challenging, and take courage and endurance to complete. Caring for ourselves, not being judgmental or harsh, and respecting our need for assurance and support, can help us to stay the course. Praying for the support of good friends, understanding teachers, and protective guides goes a long way to seeing us through this challenging time.

Prayer

Beloved Angel of Apprenticeship, teach us to accept our present situation humbly, and to do our best.
Teach us to not be harsh, critical, or too demanding of ourselves.
Rather let us benefit from our mistakes and learn to meet new challenges before becoming good at what we do.
Give us the maturity to be enough for ourselves at every level of learning.
Mastery comes with years of knowledge and practice.
Amen.

MEDITATION

Allow yourself to learn something new in life. You may find it refreshing to be in a new situation, but it might also be difficult and trying. Pat yourself on the back for being willing to meet a new challenge head-on. Transform your belief in the need always to be perfect, and give yourself the time and space to make mistakes. The way you treat yourself is indicative of how you would treat someone else who was just learning. Become a good parent to yourself: whenever you encounter a difficulty in learning, be kind to yourself. The way you treat yourself makes all the difference to how you feel about what you are doing.

Mastery flows from absolute commitment, based on passion for life.

WEEK FOUR

THE ANGEL OF MASTERY

Mastery comes from long experience, trial and error, and an absolute commitment to fulfillment. Though it may appear effortless from the outside, it can take years to attain. Masters are people who have proved themselves in the face of challenges, difficult times, and adverse conditions. They are resilient, resourceful, and respond quickly to change. They are neither rigid nor fixed in a position, but always fluid and adaptable in action and in thinking. The title "Master" itself refers to a presence that flows with energy and direction.

　　The qualities of true masters transcend age, race, gender, and social position. Their talents and skills are so developed that they can maneuver people and situations into fulfilling the goals of their own discipline and practice. Watching a master at work is inspiring. We honor all true masters, and recognize the effort and energy that went into achieving their level of development. If mastery is your goal, pursue it with all your heart.

Prayer

O, Angel of Mastery, give us the patience and humility to achieve a high level of development in our personal and professional lives.
We ask for the tenacity to persevere through trials and mistakes, and to reach a state of perfection.
We honor those who strive for mastery with respect, attention, and recognition of their focus and intent.
Amen.

MEDITATION

Focus your attention on what you would like to master in your life. Is there a goal that you are willing to give your passion and dreams to? You may become a master of living by consciously choosing a life lived from integrity, honor, and truth. A life master is God-loving and devout, a good friend, a loyal partner, and a fine person in every capacity. The mastery of life is a testament to the depth of your commitment to and love of life.

Sagittarius

ELEMENT: *Fire*

COLOR: *Blue*

RULING PLANET: *Jupiter*

FESTIVALS: *Advent*

ANGEL: *The Angel of Exploration*

Prayer

*O, Angel of Exploration,
shine your light within so that our
personal impediments evaporate
under your scrutiny.
Give us an inquisitive nature
that longs to know the hows and
whys of life.
Strengthen our appreciation of the
eternal mystery that can never be
solved, and add to our wonder at
the glory of Creation.
Amen.*

This sign, more than any other in the zodiac, produces inquisitive minds and exploring natures. The Sagittarian in us loves travel, studying, and exploring. Looking deeply within ourselves is a form of exploration that can enlighten us, and help us to understand our motivation. Knowing why we are negative, fearful, or resentful gives us an opportunity to transform ourselves and to let our light shine more brightly.

Exploration, whether of our inner nature or of the world around us, requires a willingness to take risks, to walk on the edge, and to make ourselves vulnerable. The Angel of Exploration acts as our safety net, ensuring that we do not endanger body or soul. We ask for guidance and support in opening up to new experiences that enrich our understanding. Whether we seek knowledge of the outer or the inner realm, we always come back to the Creator. All exploration is predicated on the belief that in the end we will see the light, know the goodness, and delight in our discovery that all is One.

MEDITATION

Remember the occasions when you wanted to know how things worked, or why someone did what they did. Ask yourself if that spark of inquisitiveness and exploration is still there. Allow your enthusiasm to be rekindled for knowledge of what happens to people, and things, when they are loved, cherished, and treated respectfully. Reflect on the healing power of nature, and on the profound gifts available for our use. These mysteries can awaken your dormant sense of exploration, if you will only look within.

The greatest adventure is the inner quest for spiritual treasure.

WEEK ONE

THE ANGEL OF ADVENTURE

As a species, we have met and overcome many challenges in the world of nature, and our sense of adventure is as strong as ever, our curiosity even more intense. We tend to seek out physical adventure in our youth, when our vitality is high and our inner knowing still asleep. As we mature, we begin the adventure of looking inward, and seeing how God works in and through us to transform and purify our spirit. This odyssey takes as much courage, stamina, and perseverance as conquering the outer limits of the natural world, if not more.

Going within brings a deep sense of wonder, and the excitement of discovering great treasures. Prospecting for our inner wealth is perhaps the greater adventure, because these riches can never be taken from us or spoiled in any way, other than by our conscious choice.

MEDITATION

Reflect for a moment on the adventures you have had in your life. What did you discover about yourself on these occasions? Could you see the strength and determination being required of you as you stepped away from the ordinary? Each quest for knowledge, wisdom, and inner light takes us deeper into the realm of the unknown and shows us who we are. This is true whether it is an inward journey or an outward adventure.

Prayer

O, Angel of Adventure,
help us to transform our mundane lives
into a quest for the light, joy,
and profound pleasure that come from
knowing ourselves as children of God,
which knowledge is our treasure.
Show us where exploration and discovery
reveal the inner gold of our spirits,
and where all of us
who are willing to take the risk
can venture to discover
our true selves.
Amen.

The desire for knowledge is an expression of the flame of life itself.

WEEK TWO

THE ANGEL OF CURIOSITY

Curiosity, the wholesome desire to know what life is and how it works, is natural to an open mind. When we were children we had a real sense of curiosity about life, an eager desire to be informed. Our parents and teachers tried to tame this impulse in order to keep us out of harm's way. It was channeled into learning and conformity, and often our love of adventure was discouraged.

Your sense of curiosity can be rekindled if you look into your spirit and see the flame of life burning deep within. Aren't you curious that it has never been quenched, despite all the negativity you have encountered? Aren't you eager to know more about this eternal flame that stimulates your mind, enlightens your dreams, and fires your emotions? Your curiosity is justified, because this is the Divine spark, the animus that keeps you thriving in life.

Prayer

Dearest Angel of Curiosity, ignite the spark of our minds so that we can look within and know where we have been and where our spirits long to go. Kindle our inner knowledge of the nature of the universe, the flowers that grow in spring, and the life hereafter. Help us to find answers, to surmount the limitations of body and mind, so that the way we think becomes fuller and more joyful. Amen.

MEDITATION

Take a few moments to ask yourself what you truly care about, what really matters to you. Do you need to know the small gossip of family and friends, or are you more interested in how life continues to fulfill itself on earth and in the cosmos? Find the things in your life that interest you enough to want to look more deeply into their nature. Allow your curiosity to explore these areas, and open a door to new realms of possibility.

We create our own opportunities for greater self-expression.

WEEK THREE

THE ANGEL OF OPPORTUNITY

Prayer

Beloved Angel of Opportunity,
help our light to shine, whatever our capacity.
Open our eyes to see that
what may appear as an obligation or chore
can be a window of opportunity to express
the best of ourselves.
Let us see clearly that every opportunity is
a gift that allows our light to shine.
Amen.

Opportunity presents itself when we are open to it, when we have accepted our innate goodness. It is an externalization of our inner transformation. From time to time, we are all granted windows of opportunity that allow our light to shine freely, giving us the chance to display our talents and abilities. We should be grateful for these occasions, and gladly seize the opportunity to increase the intensity of our light.

We should also recognize that these opportunities are a reflection of our own desire to expand and fulfill our potential, which takes them out of the realm of random happenings. Such opportunities do not simply happen to us: we have a personal responsibility to help create them for ourselves.

MEDITATION

Examine the essential things in your life, especially those where fear or doubt are attached. Are you willing to accept your highest good and greatest joy through them? If you are, good will come to you in opportunities for happiness and fulfillment. Consider the opportunities that have already come your way. How many did you reject out of fear that you weren't good enough, or else fail to recognize? Each moment is an opportunity to be and do your best? Say "yes" when any opportunity for self-expression and fulfillment comes your way.

Life's possibilities multiply when we risk embracing change.

WEEK FOUR

THE ANGEL OF EXPANSION

Expansion means broadening the base of our understanding and reaching deeper into the unknown realm of possibilities. Life itself demands that we push against the limitations of our minds, feelings, and physical achievements. As we extend our capabilities, our spirit grows and rejoices at its new-found expansion of being.

Our horizons broaden when we stretch ourselves in fulfilling our potential. In order to expand the dimensions of what is possible in our lives, however, we have to be willing to leave the comfort of the familiar and to step into the unknown. Holding us back are the forces of inertia: habit, the threat of change, and the fear of failure. These limit our ability to thrill to the new, and preclude the possibility of our doing anything great or wonderful. When we pause to weigh the factors for and against expanding our universe by taking real and concrete action, the result suggests that taking the plunge—growing, advancing, and moving forward—is overwhelmingly worth the risk.

MEDITATION

When we accept our limitations in a realistic way and still expand our vision of new possibilities, we live in the realm of visionary thinking. You can expand your life by embracing new possibilities. Feel worthy of the good you say you want. Say "yes" to your desire to enjoy more of life. Reflect on the thought that the more you are willing to conceive of the possibility of good things coming to you, the more room there is in your heart and mind for this to happen.

Prayer

*Sweet Angel of
Expansion,
we secretly call to
you each time we get
stuck or feel
constricted.
We ask you to expand
our sense of self
sufficiently for risk-
taking to feel natural.
Expand our
awareness that God
is always looking out
for us,
and free us to enjoy
life more.
Amen.*

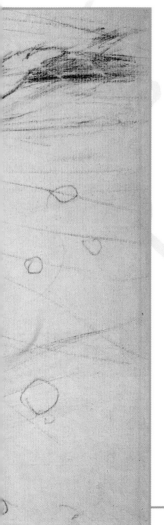

 Winter

Winter is the time of darkness, rest and recuperation. It gives us the opportunity to turn inward and connect with our inner light.

The winter solstice, about December 21, is ruled by the Archangel Gabriel, The Angel of the Word of God.

In winter we have the opportunity to experience the depths of our individuality and find our inner strength and hidden resources. As the days shorten and the sun disappears, we do less, sleep more, and journey within to both tap and replenish the core of our being. This is a time of faith, affirmation, and clear intent. We have time to focus on our actions, our relationships, and the things we care about.

We can use this quiet time to create a rich inner world where we affirm our faith in the light within. The paths of meditation and visualization take us into the realm of the subconscious mind, to the unconscious place where our dreams are woven from the fabric of our desires. Here our hopes create a tapestry for a full, rich life.

This is the time to dream the great dream of our lives. It is a creative time in which to restore our inner light by focusing our minds and devoting ourselves to God.

A Prayer for Peace

*Beloved Gabriel,
who brings us God's Strength,
help us to express our highest truths.
When we are confronted with silence or
complicity, teach us to share.
Be our guardian when we give voice to our
feelings and share our innermost thoughts.
Guide those who can make a difference
in our world.
Give us command over speech,
so that we may express the greater glory
of the Divine.
Amen.*

MEDITATION

Reflect on your freedom to speak. This is one of the most important and precious rights we have. When we suppress the truth we implode energy in our bodies, which, if held in, can poison and create fear in us. How deeply do you value your right to speak out and share your opinions, feelings, and ideas? Call on Gabriel each time you have the chance to speak your truth, and share in the higher glory of God. He will help you to express what is in your mind and heart.

The Archangel Gabriel

Gabriel is the second-highest-ranking angel in Judaism, Christianity, and Islam. His name means "God is my strength," and he is the messenger of Divine comfort. Gabriel is the Angel of the Annunciation, who revealed to the Blessed Virgin Mary that she would bear a child who would be the son of God. He is also known as the Angel of the Resurrection, of Mercy, Vengeance, Death, and Revelation.

Gabriel rules over Paradise, in the first level of heaven. He is said to sit on the left-hand side of God. In Islam, he is the "faithful spirit" and the "one terrible in power" who revealed the entire Koran to Mohammed, and who guided him one starry night to heaven. In Judaism, Gabriel is also the Prince of Fire, who destroyed the cities of Sodom and Gomorrah with fire and brimstone.

Gabriel is credited with great miracles in all three traditions. In the testimony of Joan of Arc, it was he who appeared to her and inspired her to go to the aid of the king of France. He is also thought to be the Angel of the Moon, who brings mankind the gift of hope.

Gabriel represents the Word of God and symbolizes the essence of our highest truth. We turn to him whenever we are faced with the need to speak out about things we know and feel to be right. He assists all those who speak publicly and teach higher truths, such as writers, teachers, actors, priests, and healers. He brings healing to the higher centers of the mind.

	Capricorn December 21–January 19	Aquarius January 20–February 18	Pisces February 19–March 20
ELEMENT	Earth	Air	Water
COLOR	Indigo	Violet	Purple
RULING PLANET	Saturn	Saturn	Jupiter
PART OF BODY	The knees	The legs and the ankles	The feet and the toes
ANGEL	*The Angel of Wholeness*	*The Angel of Friendship*	*The Angel of Forgiveness*
FESTIVALS	CHANUKKAH *The Angel of Miracles* CHRISTMAS *The Angel of Divine Light*	CANDLEMAS *The Angel of Honor*	YOM HASHOAH *The Angel of Remembrance*

ANGEL OF THE WEEK

WEEK 1	*The Angel of Individuality*	*The Angel of Caring*	*The Angel of Sorrow*
WEEK 2	*The Angel of Choice*	*The Angel of Sharing*	*The Angel of Reconciliation*
WEEK 3	*The Angel of Commitment*	*The Angel of Loving*	*The Angel of Release*
WEEK 4	*The Angel of Freedom*	*The Angel of Brotherhood*	*The Angel of Departure*

Capricorn

ELEMENT: *Earth*

COLOR: *Indigo*

RULING PLANET: *Saturn*

FESTIVALS: *Chanukkah*
Christmas

ANGEL: *The Angel of*
Wholeness

Feelings of wholeness and integrity develop from our awareness of the Divine light at our core. At this inner level we are complete, and in choosing to connect with this sense of wholeness, we remind ourselves that we are much more than we appear to be.

People who have experienced trauma or tragedy may be affected by their situation, but they are no less whole for that. If we realize that wholeness is who we are at core, we are less at the mercy of external circumstances. Wholeness is at the bedrock of our being. To acknowledge this is to validate our spiritual foundation and to reflect God's essence into the world. We always have the choice to identify with wholeness, rather than with the fragile or damaged parts of our personality.

The sign of Capricorn promotes singularity of vision, ambition, drive, and dedication to building a better world. People born under it have the capacity for hard work, for creating solid foundations and structures, and for bringing law and order into unruly situations. The Angel of Wholeness complements this sign by softening the edges of an otherwise hard surface. It helps us to trust others to be loving, gentle, and supportive, when our rational voice may say otherwise. Part of being whole is to allow for the weak as well as the strong, to be vulnerable as well as invincible, soft as well as hard.

Prayer

*Beloved Angel of Wholeness,
help us to find our true nature.
We always have a choice in every situation to
be ourselves.
Remind us of the part within us that never
falters, and is always whole.
Shine your light on us so that we may live
from this place,
and make wholesome choices.
Amen.*

MEDITATION

Reflect on your true nature. This is the deepest place within you, which is always awake, aware, conscious, whole, healthy, and intact. Nothing can destroy this aspect of you. When you choose to know and to identify with this Divine part of yourself, you will find joy, healing, and release from the past. You can go to this place any time you feel less than whole, or less than yourself. It is where love, comfort, and all knowing exist.

Individuality is a rite of passage in which we choose to accept ourselves.

THE ANGEL OF INDIVIDUALITY

Individuality is the essence of a refined and differentiated consciousness that can place itself in the here and now as well as be part of the greater whole. Our individuality is not defined externally; it is linked unequivocally with inner self-knowledge.

Accepting our individuality means to be loving and understanding of who we have become and who we truly are. When we can say "I am that I am," we open the door to unlimited spiritual energy and, at the same time, anchor our personal identity within the higher self. To become an individual is a rite of passage, during which time we step away from the collective unconscious that rules family and community, and learn to stand firmly for what we know to be right and good. Everyone has the right to know, fundamentally, who he or she is.

Prayer

Dearest Angel of Individuality, we give thanks to you for deepening our sense of personal identity, and teaching us that we retain a boundary of uniqueness and self, while belonging to the greater good. Help us to define who we are, so that we can make conscious choices that work for us and fulfill our lives.
Amen.

MEDITATION

Reflect on the qualities that are particular to you as an individual. Are these related to your ability to speak the truth and know what you like and don't like? Your individuality is formed by what has happened to you, and how you have come to see the world. Be willing to define what makes you different from, and also what makes you the same as, others. Look at what you identify with, and consider whether it might not be pleasing or wholesome to transform the way you see yourself. You define your individuality from within.

Angels of the week

Prayer

*Beloved Angel of
Choice,
we ask you to help us
to make wholesome
choices for our lives.
Open our minds to
the things and people
that are life
enhancing, and help
us to grow.
Help us to choose
levels of development
that serve our
spirituality and
well-being.
Choice honors our
being.
Amen.*

The freedom to choose our path is an expression of our divinity.

WEEK TWO

THE ANGEL OF CHOICE

The power to exercise choice allows us to decide how we want to live and in what ways we hope to express our higher goals and aspirations. When our options are varied and the possibilities are abundant, we can fully experience our individual nature; but when our choices are limited, we are forced into a narrow, uniform mold.

The ability to choose distinguishes free people from those who are compelled, for whatever reason, to follow a path of conformity. Freedom of choice distinguishes us from the rest of the animal kingdom. We can choose the path that works for our highest good, or that which sabotages us. When we allow ourselves to be dependent upon the opinions and ideas of other people, we forfeit our freedom. Choosing is the prerogative of free adults to do their best.

MEDITATION

Reflect on your ability to make wholesome choices. Do you consciously choose what comes your way in life, embracing it and making it yours? Or do you separate yourself from what life wants you to experience and blame others for your situation? Trust in your ability to choose the people and situations that will bring about your highest good and greatest joy. You could even regard all experiences as lessons, leading you toward the path of your highest potential. Every event in life reinforces your ability to choose for yourself. This is how we discover the laws of truth.

THE ANGEL OF COMMITMENT

Commitment to ourselves and to life opens, rather than closes, doors.

Commitment is a wholehearted response that engages body, mind, and spirit. It is a magnanimous embrace that affirms life, your choices, and who you are, on every level.

Today, many people shy away from making commitments. They may believe the delusion that there is something better waiting for them, and fear losing options by committing themselves. This reluctance, in fact, reflects fear, and is a state of avoidance. When we commit ourselves, we actually place the highest part of our spirit in the service of life. Commitment creates a safe space in which healing and wholeness can occur. When we are only half engaged, our heart aches to give and receive more. Commitment sets us on the road to growth and self-discovery.

Prayer

O Angel of Commitment, sharpen our commitment to life, so that we are free to be our best and to give from the depths of our heart. When we avoid the fullness of being present, we cheat ourselves of the opportunity to discover who we truly are. Help us to work through fear and immature ideas, so that we can stand firmly and give wholeheartedly. Amen.

MEDITATION

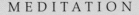

Reflect on the commitments you have made. Look at your commitment to your relationships, your work, your health, happiness, and spiritual growth. Can you make a commitment to live from the highest principles of love and joy? Living from a commitment to honor yourself, no matter what, will teach you to listen and to pay attention to God speaking within you. The more deeply you honor yourself, the fuller and richer your life becomes. When you can commit to yourself, you can make a true commitment to others.

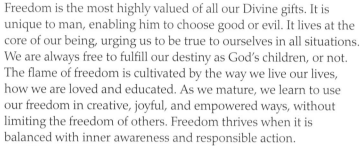

*Freedom is our
most precious gift.
It enables us to
fulfill our purpose.*

WEEK FOUR

THE ANGEL
OF FREEDOM

Freedom is the most highly valued of all our Divine gifts. It is unique to man, enabling him to choose good or evil. It lives at the core of our being, urging us to be true to ourselves in all situations. We are always free to fulfill our destiny as God's children, or not. The flame of freedom is cultivated by the way we live our lives, how we are loved and educated. As we mature, we learn to use our freedom in creative, joyful, and empowered ways, without limiting the freedom of others. Freedom thrives when it is balanced with inner awareness and responsible action.

We need to be free to make mistakes, to change our minds later, even to see the error of our ways. God would not ask us to come to Him in any other way than by choosing freely.

Prayer

*O, Angel of Freedom,
guide us to know full well your power
to transform our lives.
Lead us into freedom,
and away from the bondage of enslaved
thinking and living.
Teach us to be responsible for our actions,
and to guard against corruption.
Let freedom radiate from
the core of our being.
Amen.*

MEDITATION

Reflect on a time you were forced to make an important decision about your life, or the lives of others. You knew that, although there were many considerations, ultimately there was only one correct choice. Are you aware that your decision, even though it may have been difficult or painful to reach, came from the depths of your being? This is the place in you that loves and values freedom. Acknowledge this part of yourself that freely chose to be responsible, to do the best for yourself and those in your care. Give thanks for the freedom to choose your path in life. Our choices may not always appear right to others, but they come from the light deep within us that yearns for freedom.

Aquarius

ELEMENT: *Air*

COLOR: *Violet*

RULING PLANET: *Saturn*

FESTIVALS: *Candlemas*

ANGEL: *The Angel of Friendship*

Friendship can satisfy our deep desire for love and acceptance. What we value most in ourselves is reflected in our friendships with others. We often see our humor, truth, and beauty reflected in them. They show us our light, joy, vulnerability, and fragility, and enable us to fulfill our longing to bond with someone who understands and cherishes us. Healthy friendships are based on accepting differences and giving others the freedom to be who they are without feeling a need to change them. Friendships that are mutually supportive bring out the best in us, and are based on love of spirit and wholesome values. A good friendship withstands separation and the passing of time.

Few signs have the gift of friendship as strongly aspected in the zodiac as Aquarius. Openness of mind, a gracious spirit, idealism, responsibility, clear analytical thinking, and generosity bring acceptance, insight, and love to a relationship. When you are in need of a friend, ask the Angel of Friendship to bring a worthy soul into your life. Know that you are deserving of friends who see the light within you, and who love and honor you for who you are.

MEDITATION

Think of those people in your life who befriended you in times of change and transition. Bless them, and in so doing open your heart and mind to the meaning of friendship. Be thankful for the friends who see you in a loving light, who believe in you, and who remain on your side, regardless of what you do. Find room in your heart for the friends of your youth, your current friends, and the friends who supported you in times of change. Be a good friend to yourself through all the ups and downs of life.

Prayer

O, Angel of Friendship, send us good relationships that can withstand differences in personalities as well as the separation of time and distance.

Friendship is a wonderful experience in times of pain or need, and a blessing in times of joy and thriving.

Let us be thankful for present friends, and also make room for new people in our lives.

We seek kindred spirits who reflect the best in ourselves, and who are able to join in the sharing we call friendship.

Amen.

The caring response of a warm heart is happily infectious.

WEEK ONE

THE ANGEL OF CARING

When we care about people, we focus our feelings and thoughts on them in a way that brings them into our lives. We engage our heart with their lives and their concerns, so that what they do and what happens to them affects us. Caring isn't a question of fixing or doing, but of directing our intentions toward a positive outcome for those we care about.

Allowing yourself to care means that you have been touched by life. The ability to care reflects an open heart and a capacity to feel and respond to what goes on around you. Caring is a sign that you are human, that your values are real, and based on a deep sense of truth, rather than on the superficial, materialistic norms of modern society. Caring people warm our hearts and invite us to find the place within ourselves where we, too, can be caring. You will always feel good about yourself for caring. It is a sign of a full heart and compassion.

Prayer

*Beloved Angel of Caring,
you bring caring close to our hearts, and deepen and enrich every aspect of our relationship with others.
Care is what binds us to people and things; it makes the difference when we feel separated or fragile.
To know that we are cared for, and can open our hearts to care for others, is what makes us eternally lovable and infinitely human.
Amen.*

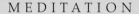

MEDITATION

Reflect on what you care about deeply in life. Remember those who care about you, and offer a prayer for their healing and happiness. You can show your care through encouragement and support for the things that matter to them. Care opens your heart and fills it with compassion, whether for people, animals, or a cause. Care can ennoble you. It brings the angels close to you, for they care deeply about things. Caring is one of the greatest gifts you extend to the world; it reflects your humanity and makes you more like the angels.

Angels of the week

Sharing is the expression and proof of love and interconnectedness.

Prayer

O, Angel of Sharing, grant us ease in sharing the best of ourselves with others. Help us to feel safe showing our talents, gifts, and insights, and to experience the sweet joy of giving. Allow us to know the kindness of others who share themselves with warmth, and who invite us to give of our own goodness. Teach us how to give, and show us the true value of participating with others. Amen.

WEEK TWO

THE ANGEL OF SHARING

To what degree are you able or willing to share the best of yourself? Are you aware of other people sharing themselves with you? The act of sharing can be a social experience, in which we literally share our wealth, material possessions, or food; it can also be an emotional experience, where we share with others the inner reality of our feelings, our thoughts, and ideas.

Sharing is how we acknowledge that we are part of a greater whole. No man, or woman, is an island. Be willing to share more of yourself with others, and you will experience a deep connection with the world. You will feel the rewards of giving in the reciprocal warmth and openness of the people around you. This new-found mutuality will bring home to you the powerful realization that you are a part of the heart of life.

MEDITATION

Think about how you share with others. Do you give of your best? Your way of sharing might simply be to be with the people you know, love, and trust. Do you share your gifts with people who are in need? Sharing is always a two-way experience, and in many cases you get back much more than you give. Reflect on what you feel when sharing. First, a space opens in your heart and mind for you to give and to receive. Next, you find that you are comfortable sharing with others to a limited extent. Then, when next you have the opportunity, you discover that you are capable of giving much more.

Love starts with ourselves and radiates out toward others.

WEEK THREE

THE ANGEL OF LOVING

Loving others involves communication and warmth. It is an invitation received, acknowledged, and enjoyed. Loving is a way of being together without fear of rejection or pain. It is a joyful communion with those who warm our hearts. We are loving when we resonate with our inner reality, pacing ourselves so that we have time to listen to our hearts and know what we are feeling. Loving starts with how we treat ourselves, and radiates out to others.

MEDITATION

Being loving means leaving judgment behind, and accepting ourselves and other people completely. It means treating ourselves and others in the warmest, kindest, and most compassionate way possible. Reflect on your ability to love, first yourself and then others. You can choose to be loving whenever you feel welcome, safe, and accepted. Give yourself permission to feel this way. It feeds your soul when you are loving and experience the love of others.

Prayer

*Beloved Angel of Loving,
bring us the warmth of shared feelings, of gentle touch, laughter, and humor.
Show us that by loving we radiate kindness, tenderness, and respect for ourselves and for others.
Show us how to let our defenses down and become the loving person we know we are.
Warm our hearts, and help us to stabilize our sense of self in the world by acting in a loving manner.
Amen.*

A sense of shared humanity rewards the giving and receiving of gifts.

WEEK FOUR

THE ANGEL OF BROTHERHOOD

Brotherhood, the feeling of unity with humankind, comes from being aligned with those around us in harmony, joy, and peace. We experience joy when we share our talents, knowledge, desires, and endeavors with others. These mutual relationships are where we bond, form deep allegiances, and come to know ourselves better through sharing.

A sense of brotherhood lets us feel that we have a worthy place, and that we belong to the greater whole. Brotherhood teaches us the oneness of life; it helps us to realize that we are a single human family, sharing the planet.

MEDITATION

Do you remember a time when you were young and desperately wanted a friend? You may have been lonely, or new at school, or in the neighborhood. Do you remember someone who reached out a hand in friendship? It is said that to have a good friend you need to be a good friend.

Allow your warmth and kindness to express itself in friendship, even momentarily, to someone else in need. Think of the people around you now, in your college, neighborhood, or workplace. Could you, in your turn, extend a helping hand in a gentle, unobtrusive way to someone in need? Experience their gratitude and happiness reflected back to you. Allow this act of brotherhood to become an ingrained part of your relationship with others.

Prayer

Beloved Angel of Brotherhood, join us with our sisters and brothers in the shared ideals of healing. Let us help one another. Know that who we are is defined by our relationship with ourselves, with one another, and, ultimately, with God. Unite us in our common purpose of fulfilling our highest potential in an arena of sharing, bonding, and love. Amen.

Pisces

ELEMENT: *Water*

COLOR: *Purple*

RULING PLANET: *Jupiter*

FESTIVALS: *Yom Hashoah*

ANGEL: *The Angel of Forgiveness*

Forgiveness is the single greatest act we can perform. It sets us free, cleans the slate, and releases negativity. Hatred, resentment, and spite weigh heavily upon us, limiting our life force and stunting our emotions. People stuck in hatred have unhappy lives, and are often affected by illness. Forgiveness brings our consciousness closer to God and His angels, who forgive us even when we cannot forgive ourselves. There is nothing that God will not forgive, should the pardon be sought. We have only to purify our hearts, and to allow His grace and forgiveness to touch us. When we forgive ourselves, we free our minds, lighten our hearts, and repair the damage to our fragile psyches. When we forgive those who have injured us, we reclaim our dignity and power. Forgiveness helps us to retrieve pieces of our soul that have slipped away in acts of abuse or malice.

The Angel of Forgiveness is eager to bring us healing, and to help us to find the grace to forgive those who have hurt us. The act of forgiveness, whether for ourselves or for others, cleanses our wounds and purifies our souls.

MEDITATION

Reflect for a moment on the people in your life who are in need of forgiveness. You may never understand why they behaved the way they did toward you. Yet you know that in your heart you carry a dark cloud of resentment or bitterness about them. In forgiving them, you take your power back. By forgiving yourself, you restore your own self-image. Releasing your negativity toward others is part of the purification process in which you free yourself of the burdens of your heart. Forgiveness makes you whole and complete. Allow yourself to experience it.

Prayer

Beloved Angel of
Forgiveness,
you bring us the
answer of redemption
when we forgive the
hurt and abuse of the
past.
Teach us the
significance of
forgiving others,
and show us that this
is where healing
begins.
Allow us to forgive
ourselves for not
being what we
thought we should be.
Show us that
forgiveness leads
directly to opening up
and purifying our
hearts,
and allows healing to
happen.
Amen.

Angels of the week

*Acknowledgment
of our sorrow can
help to restore
the spirit.*

WEEK ONE

THE ANGEL
OF SORROW

180

Sorrow runs deeper than any other emotion. No one is spared it in life, but a strong spiritual context can help to contain it and give us the strength to carry on. If we allow ourselves to feel the pain of our grief when it wells up, and to weep, this connects us with what is real and deep within us, and helps lighten the burden. To dwell on sorrow, however, is to ignore the present moment, and to suppress our life force. By honoring our feelings when they arise, we respect the moment, redeem our spirit, and soften our hearts.

Prayer

*Dear Angel of Sorrow,
you have shown us how to transcend
our grief and lessen our sorrow through
expressing our feelings.
Open our hearts to the experience of loss,
and free the unshed tears that
weigh our spirit down.
Help us to release the pain that
limits our experience of this
most precious gift of life.
Amen.*

MEDITATION

Reflect on the experiences that are the source of your sorrow. Can you release your attachment to them, put them behind you, and find new ways of living in the present? In the now are all the tools you need for healing the wounds of the past. Here are the balm of forgiveness and the gratitude for life's goodness that will assuage your sorrow and enable you to receive the healing you need for the life ahead of you.

*Reconciliation
with the past
brings freedom to
live in the present.*

WEEK TWO

THE ANGEL OF RECONCILIATION

Reconciliation is the acceptance, at a deep level of consciousness, of what has happened in the past and of what remains unfulfilled in the present. Once we have recognized that things are the way they are, whether we like it or not, we are able to come to terms with pain, loss, and separation. We can acknowledge the lost opportunities, unfulfilled promises, and disappointing outcomes, say goodbye to the past, and move on with our lives.

This is a cleansing process that brings us into the here and now, where we can take the next step forward. When we are reconciled to our lot in life, we appreciate the good things we have, and how valuable the present is for experiencing love, friendship, and joy. Reconciliation brings completion and closure, so that we are free to enjoy the hope and promise of tomorrow.

Prayer

*Dearest Angel of Reconciliation,
help us to be grateful for all that we
have in our lives.
Show us that it is safe to release the past,
bury our pain and sorrow, and live in
the joy of today.
Memories of love warm our hearts and
help to reconcile us to the loss of
those we have cherished.
Help us to live more fully in the present
as we accept life.
Reconciliation sets us free.
Amen.*

MEDITATION

Reflect on whatever remains unreconciled in your heart. To find completion and live fully in the present, you need to accept all that has happened in your past, no matter how painful. When you accept the past, you will develop wisdom and a perspective that allows you to see the good and bad of any situation. For every situation has its golden and dark moments. Reconciliation strengthens your spiritual context by realistically affirming the present, and by acknowledging your vulnerability and your strengths. It creates a quality of emotional stability that sustains you, and allows you to start the healing process now.

*Release from
negative feelings
opens new doors to
life and goodness.*

Prayer

*Dear Angel of Release,
teach us to let go of what fails to
serve our growth or healing.
Living in the light of God's love, help us
to release old, negative thinking.
Teach us the importance of release in
preparation for the moment of death,
when we let go of this earthly life
to live in eternal bliss
with God.
Amen.*

WEEK THREE

THE ANGEL
OF RELEASE

Release is the inner work needed to live joyfully in the present. When we tie up our emotions, we limit our vitality and weigh down our spirit. By releasing doubts, fears, and painful feelings, we reclaim our power and emerge vital and overflowing with life. Emotional release entails acknowledging and expressing anger, rage, betrayal, hurt, or the wish that things might have been different. Knowing that you have a right to your feelings permits you to experience them. Once you allow yourself to express your emotions, you open the door to healing and forgiveness. Without release you remain blocked, and your energy is stuck in the past. When you let go of negativity and experience the richness of your feelings, you are actually choosing life.

MEDITATION

Release all the stale ideas and oppressive feelings about yourself and life that limit you. To let go of these negative emotions, you have to be able to feel and express them fully. Do this in a safe place, where you will have the privacy to shout, scream, or cry undisturbed. Every experience was designed by the higher self to bring about expanded awareness and refined consciousness. Releasing your pent-up feelings will open the door to peace and vitality. You will have given your perceptions the opportunity to change, and it will be easier to create a spiritual context for your experiences. You may find that you are able to bring wisdom, forgiveness, and clarity to your situation.

Departure from this life is but a stage on the soul's great journey.

WEEK FOUR

THE ANGEL OF DEPARTURE

All of us must make the homeward journey, back to God. The way we think about this journey affects the manner of our departure. Looking at death with fear and trepidation makes our leave-taking painful and fraught with tension. Understanding that nothing on this earth is permanent, however, enables us to live our lives more fully, and to accept what is inevitable.

Once we realize that we have a limited time in which to fulfill our promise and share the best of ourselves, our fear and negative feelings vanish. Acceptance of the Divine plan becomes the basis for living in preparation for our own departure. The Angel of Departure heals our spirit so that it can return peacefully to God, in order to bring healing to other realms of existence.

Prayer

O, Beloved Angel of Departure,
help us to accept the temporal nature of life,
and realize that we do not have forever to
fulfill our gifts or love those
who are close to us.
Teach us that life is to be lived now,
in the moment, when we can feel love and
share our gratitude.
Open our hearts to one another,
shine your light upon our spirits, and bless us
with an easy departure from this
earthly plane.
Amen.

MEDITATION

How you would use your time and energy if you had only a few days more to live? Who would you share your love with? Who would you thank for their friendship and support? What would you long to experience once more? Generally, people in this extreme situation raise their awareness and make the very best of their remaining time. Their quality of life is rich and positive. They forgive, reconcile what they can, and say their goodbyes graciously. You can learn from this example by imagining your own departure, and realizing what in your life has been left undone or needs to be put right.

Angel Index

Acknowledgments

My special thanks to my editor, Geoffrey Chesler, who helped in the conception and development of this book. He insisted on clarification, precision, and grounding: that I dot my "I"s and cross my "T"s, both metaphorically and in reality. Our working relationship has endured changes of home, job, and country, and led to a deepening spiritual perspective, I believe, on both our parts over time.

My thanks to my friend and agent Susan Mears, to Elizabeth Rice at Hearst Books, and to Amy Carroll and Denise Brown of Carroll & Brown for the beautiful design and production that makes this book so rich. You have all been working angels whom any writer would be glad to have on her side.

Writing about angels in the midst of change was good for my heart and soul. It reminded me to call for the help I needed at the time, and to be ever grateful for the love, guidance, and protection I am eternally offered.

To the earth angels in my new home of Boulder, Colorado, who have helped to make this transition a daily task of connecting and grounding my spirit: to Judy Jones, for the wisdom, good walks and friendship; to Mikki Brooks, for a kind and understanding presence that was constant during adjustment and change; to Fawn Christianson, for long phone talks and real, grounded assistance in getting my work "out there"; to my cousin, Tani Cohen, for supportive, daily e-mails to see how I was getting on; to Kathy Owen, for friendship and always helping me to put life in a healthy perspective; to Olivia Dewhurst-Maddox and Lady Mary Jardine, for kindness and love that I trust will endure; to Ann Macfarlane, for helping me to form a workable, everyday spirituality; to all of you, my thanks.

My thanks to God in Heaven and His angels for a safe return to my homeland after thirty years away, for this special opportunity to express myself, and for the healing and peace that have come with writing this book.

God bless us all.

AMBIKA WAUTERS

Bibliography

Attwater, Donald. *The Penguin Dictionary of Saints*. Harmondsworth, Middlesex: Penguin Books, 1975.

Ben Shimon Halevy, Ze'ev. *Kabbalah, The Divine Plan*. San Francisco: HarperSanFrancisco, 1996.

Boros, Ladislaus. *Angels and Men*. London: Search Press, 1974.

Brandon, S. G. F. (ed.). *A Dictionary of Comparative Religion*. New York: Charles Scribner's Sons, 1970.

Burnham, Sophie. *A Book of Angels*. New York: Ballantine Books,1990.

Connolly, David. *In Search of Angels*. New York: Putnam Publishing, 1993.

Cross, F. L. (ed.). *The Oxford Dictionary of the Christian Church*. London: Oxford University Press, 1966.

Cowie, L. W. and John Selwyn Gummer. *The Christian Calendar*. London: Weidenfeld and Nicolson, 1974.

Davidson, Gustav. *A Dictionary of Angels*. New York: The Free Press, 1967.

Mallasz, Gitta. *Talking with Angels*. Einsiedeln, Switzerland: Daimon Verlag, 1992.

Metford, J. C. J. *The Christian Year*. London: Thames and Hudson, 1991.

Moolenburgh, H. C. *A Handbook of Angels*. Saffron Walden, Essex: The C. W. Daniel Company, 1988.

Ruthven, Malise. *Islam, A Very Short Introduction*. Oxford/New York: Oxford University Press, 1997.

Steiner, Rudolf. *The Spiritual Hierarchies*. New York: Anthroposophic Press, 1970.

Steiner, Rudolf. *Angel*. London: The Rudolf Steiner Press, 1996.

Synnestvedt, Sig. *The Essential Swedenborg*. New York: The Swedenborg Foundation, 1970.

Szekely, Edmond Bordeaux. *The Gospel of the Essenes*. Saffron Walden, Essex: The C.W. Daniel Company, 1979.

Unterman, Alan. *Dictionary of Jewish Lore and Legend*. London: Thames and Hudson, 1991.

Wauters, Ambika. *The Angel Oracle*. New York: St. Martin's Press, 1995.

Picture Credits

pages 2 & 107 *Angel Playing a Harp* (detail from an Altarpiece of the Virgin of the Aballa Conca) by Pere Serra (fl.1357–1405). Museo Diocesano de Lerida, Catalonia, Spain/Index/Bridgeman Art Library

8 Mary Evans Picture Library

9 Museo Trident Arte Sacra Trento/The Art Archive

10 *The Guardian Angels* by Joshua Hargrave Sams Mann (fl.1849-85). Haynes Fine Art at the Bindery Galleries, Broadway/Bridgeman Art Library

13 British Library/The Art Archive

15 Biblioteca dell'Escorial, Spain/The Art Archive

17 *Young Girls Dancing at Shavuot*, 1997 (oil on canvas) by Dora Holzhandler (contemporary artist). Private Collection/Bridgeman Art Library

19 Mary Evans Picture Library

21 Moses and the burning bush; Moses taking the family back to Egypt; Moses meeting Aaron; Moses and Aaron before Pharaoh, *Golden Haggadah*, 1320. British Library, London, UK/Bridgeman Art Library

23 Angel, from the *Presentation of Christ in the Temple*, *c.*1305 (fresco) by Giotto di Bondone (*c.*1266–1337). Scrovegni Chapel, Padua, Italy/Bridgeman Art Library

25 Robert Harding Picture Library

27 *Adoration of an Angel* (panel) by Fra Angelico (Guido di Pietro) (*c.*1387–1455). Louvre, Paris, France/Bridgeman Art Library

29 An Angel, from the *Coronation of the Virgin*, completed 1454 by Enguerrand Quarton (*c.*1410–66). Villeneuve-les-Avignon (Hospice), Anjou, France/Giraudon/Bridgeman Art Library

31 *Archangel Michael* by Guariento de Arpo (fl. 1350–1400). Museo Bottacin e Museo Civico, Italy/Bridgeman Art Library

32 Biblioteca dell'Escorial Spain/The Art Archive

35 *Rothschild Canticles* (MS404)/Beinecke Rare Books and Manuscripts Library/Yale University.

36 St. Mark's Cathedral/The Art Archive

38 Imperial War Museum/The Art Archive

41 Mary Evans Picture Library

43 *Two Angels* (drawing) by Giovanni Battista Cipriani (1727–85). Victoria & Albert Museum, London, UK/Bridgeman Art Library

45 Mary Evans Picture Library

47 *Angel Beating a Drum*, detail from the Linaivoli Triptych, 1433 (tempera on panel) by Fra Angelico (Guido di Pietro) (*c.*1387–1455). Museo di San Marco dell'Angelico, Florence, Italy/Bridgeman Art Library

49 *Head of an Angel*, after Rembrandt, 1889 by Vincent van Gogh (1853–90). Private Collection/Bridgeman Art Library

51 Anagni Cathedral, Italy/The Art Archive

53 *The Golden Cell*, 1892 (oil and gold metallic paint on paper) by Odilon Redon (1840–1916). British Museum, London, UK/Bridgeman Art Library

54 San Vitale Ravenna, Italy/The Art Archive

57 Beaux Arts Museum Rouen/The Art Archive

59 Mary Evans Picture Library

60 AKG Photo, London

61 Suermondt Museum, Aachen/The Art Archive

63 & 95 Angels in a heavenly landscape, the right hand wall of the apse, from the *Journey of the Magi* cycle in the chapel, *c.*1460 (fresco) by Benozzo di Lese di Sandro Gozzoli (1420–97). Palazzo Medici-Riccardi, Florence, Italy/Bridgeman Art Library

64 Galleria degli Uffizi, Florence/The Art Archive

66 Louvre, Paris/The Art Archive

68 Scrovegni Chapel, Padua/The Art Archive

70 *The Cloister or the World*, 1896 by Arthur Hacker (1858–1919). Bradford Art Galleries and Museums, West Yorkshire, UK/Bridgeman Art Library

73 *The Angel of the Trumpet* by Sir Edward Burne-Jones (1833–98). The Makins Collection/Bridgeman Art Library

74 Angels in a heavenly landscape, the left hand wall of the apse, from the *Journey of the Magi* cycle in the chapel, *c.*1460 (fresco) by Benozzo di Lese di Sandro Gozzoli (1420–97). Palazzo Medici-Riccardi, Florence, Italy/Bridgeman Art Library

76 *Two Angels* by Charles Francois Sellier (1830-82) Private Collection/Bridgeman Art Library

79 *St. Nicholas of Tolentino with a Concert of Angels* by Ambroise Fredeau (1589–1673). Musée des Augustins, Toulouse, France/Giraudon/Bridgeman Art Library

81 *Angeli Laudantes* tapestry designed by Henry Dearle with figures by Sir Edward Burne-Jones originally drawn in 1877/78, woven at Merton Abbey in 1894 by Morris and Co. (wool & silk on cotton). Victoria & Albert Museum, London, UK/Bridgeman Art Library

82 *The Annunciation* (detail of an angel) by Jacopo Pontormo (1494–1557). Capponi Chapel, Santa Felicita, Florence, Italy/Bridgeman Art Library

85 *Musical Angels*, relief from the Cantoria by Luca della Robbia (1400–82), *c.*1435 (marble). Museo dell'Opera del Duomo, Florence, Italy/Bridgeman Art Library

87 Mary Evans Picture Library
89 *A Concert of Angels* by Spanish School (16th century). Museo de Bellas Artes, Bilbao, Spain/Index/Bridgeman Art Library
91 Mary Evans Picture Library
92 AKG Photo, London
93 Mary Evans Picture Library
96 Mary Evans Picture Library
99 The Ancient Art & Architecture Collection
100 *Three Trumpeting Angels* designed by Sir Edward Burne-Jones, executed by Morris Marshall Faulkner and Co. South aisle window, Edward the Confessor Church, Cheddleton, Staffordshire, UK/Bridgeman Art Library
102 National Gallery, London/The Art Archive
105 Angels from the *Santa Trinita Altarpiece* by Giovanni Cimabue (1240–1302). Galleria degli Uffizi, Florence, Italy/Bridgeman Art Library
108 *Three Angels* (panel) by Ridolfo Ghirlandaio II (Bigordi) (1483–1561). Galleria dell'Accademia, Florence, Italy/Bridgeman Art Library
110 Angels from the *Madonna della Melagrana* by Sandro Botticelli (1444/5–1510). Galleria degli Uffizi, Florence, Italy/Bridgeman Art Library
112 Civicche Raccolte d'Arte, Verona Castellvecchio/The Art Archive
115 *Study of the Head of an Angel* (chalk on paper) by Andrea del Verrocchio (1435–88). Gabinetto dei Disegni e Stampe, Galleria degli Uffizi, Florence, Italy/Bridgeman Art Library
116 *Angel* by Sir Edward Burne-Jones (1833–98). Private Collection/Bridgeman Art Library
118 *Vallombrosa Altarpiece*, detail of Angel Musicians by Pietro Perugino (c.1445–1523). Galleria dell'Accademia, Florence, Italy/Bridgeman Art Library
120 David Murray
123 British Library/The Art Archive
125 Mary Evans Picture Library
126 *The Archangel Michael*, from a triptych by Hans Memling (c.1433–94). Christie's Images, London, UK/Bridgeman Art Library
127 National Gallery, Siena/The Art Archive
128 Dominican Church Bolzano/The Art Archive
130 Prado, Madrid/The Art Archive
133 Museo del Duomo, Friuli/The Art Archive
134 Civic Museum, Udine/The Art Archive
137 Minstrel angel playing a lute, detail from *The Presentation of Jesus in the Temple*, 1510 (panel) by Vittore Carpaccio (c.1460/5–1523/6). Galleria dell'Accademia, Venice, Italy/Bridgeman Art Library
138 Royal Fine Art Museum, Antwerp/The Art Archive
140 Angel musicians, detail from the right hand side of the *Ghent Altarpiece*, 1432 (panel) by Hubert Eyck (c.1370–1426) & Jan van Eyck (1390–1441). St. Bavo Cathedral, Ghent, Belgium/Giraudon/Bridgeman Art Library
143 Prado, Madrid/The Art Archive
144 Detail of an angel from *The Annunciation to the Shepherds*, 1656 by Nicolaes Pietersz. Berchem (1620–83). Bristol City Museum and Art Gallery, UK/Bridgeman Art Library
147 Raft of Cherubs, from the *Gallery of Maps*, commissioned by Gregory XIII between 1580–83 (detail) by Egnazio Danti (1536–86). Vatican Museums and Galleries, Vatican City, Italy/Bridgeman Art Library
149 Rheinisches Landesmuseum, Bonn/The Art Archive
150 Detail of angels from the *Altarpiece of San Barnaba* by Sandro Botticelli (1444/5–1510). Galleria degli Uffizi, Florence, Italy/Bridgeman Art Library
153 Basilica Aquileia, Italy/The Art Archive
154 *An Angel Striding Among the Stars* (drawing) by William Blake (1757–1827). Victoria & Albert Museum, London, UK/Bridgeman Art Library
157 Diocesan Museum, Cortona, Italy/The Art Archive
158 & 159 *The Annunciation* by Giuseppe Velásquez (b.1540). Rafael Valls Gallery, London, UK/Bridgeman Art Library
161 *The Annunciation* by Filippino Lippi (c.1457–1504). Galleria dell'Accademia, Florence, Italy/Bridgeman Art Library
163 *An Angel holding a Glass Flask* by Juan de Valdes Leal (1622–90) (studio of). Phillips, The International Fine Art Auctioneers, UK/Bridgeman Art Library
164 Scrovegni Chapel, Padua/The Art Archive
166 Cuenca Cathedral, Spain/The Art Archive
169 Scrovegni Chapel, Padua/The Art Archive
171 National Gallery, London/The Art Archive
172 *The Angel of Life* by Giovanni Segantini (1858–99). Civica Galleria d'Arte Moderna, Milan, Italy/Bridgeman Art Library
174 *Christ Served by the Angels* by Jacques de Stella (1596–1657). Galleria degli Uffizi, Florence, Italy/Bridgeman Art Library
177 Robert Harding Picture Library
179 Victoria & Albert Museum/The Art Archive
180/181 Angels, from the *Lamentation, c.*1305 (fresco) by Giotto di Bondone (c.1266–1337). Scrovegni Chapel, Padua, Italy/Bridgeman Art Library
183 *Out of the deep* by Phoebe Traquair/National Museums of Scotland
184 Turkish/Islamic Art Museum, Istanbul/The Art Archive
187 *Jacob's Ladder* by William Blake (1757–1827). British Museum, London, UK/Bridgeman Art Library